LES MISERABLES

A Full-Length Drama
adapted by
TIM KELLY
from the novel by
Victor Hugo

THE DRAMATIC PUBLISHING COMPANY

*** NOTICE ***

LES MISÉRABLES

A Play in Two Acts
For a flexible cast of 30 players*

CHARACTERS
(in order of speaking)

VICTOR H* .... narrator
THENARDIER .... an evil man
MME. THENARDIER .... his unpleasant wife
EPONINE .... their daughter
AZELMA .... a younger daughter
CHAMPMATHIEU .... a simpleton accused of being Valjean
JEAN VALJEAN .... ex-convict
MME. MAGLIORE .... townswoman
MONSEIGNEUR MYRIEL .... kindly priest
MLLE. BAPTISTINE .... his talkative sister
SERGEANT .... of the police
POLICEMAN .... his partner
FANTINE .... young mother
MME. VICTURIEN .... busybody, in charge of bead factory
FAUCHELEVENT* .... townsman
GIRL #1 .... factory worker
GIRL #2 .... factory worker
GIRL #3 .... factory worker
MARGUERITE .... flower girl
INSPECTOR JAVERT .... police inspector
BAMATABOIS .... unpleasant young man
JUDGE .... conducts trial
PROSECUTOR .... determined to convict

MME. RONDEAU .... witness against Champmathieu
MME. GRIBIER .... gossip
SISTER SIMPLICITY .... hospital nun
MARIUS .... in love with Cosette
MLLE. GILLENORMAND ... his aunt, an elderly aristocrat
ADELE .... student
HENRI* .... student
COSETTE .... Fantine's daughter
CHARLOTTE .... housekeeper

NON-SPEAKING "bits" (easily doubled): Young Man,
Young Woman, Prisoner Bibolet, Wedding Guests, Citizens.

For 16 women and 14 men. Can also be 17, 18, 19 women and
11, 12, 13 men. Much smaller with doubling. Optional extras.

*These roles can be switched to female. CONSULT FLEXIBLE
CASTING IN PRODUCTION NOTES.

TIME: 19th Century, covers period of 15 years.

PLACE: France.

STORY OF THE PLAY

"LES MISÉRABLES", one of the world's great literary classics, sold out its first edition the day it went on sale in 1862. Since then it has never been out of print, has been filmed countless times and is currently the subject of a smash hit international pop-opera.

This gripping new version has been designed for very simple production needs (basically a few tables, chairs and a bench). Under two hours. It's the story of ex-convict, Jean Valjean, and his relentless pursuit by "law and order" police Inspector Javert. Filled with fascinating vignettes of 19th Century France, the script boasts a brilliant cast of characters who weave an exciting tapestry of humankind at its best and worst.

Special emphasis has been placed on the many small roles and female characters -- the tragic Fantine and her daughter Cosette, the wretched Madame Thenardier, the lovelorn Eponine -- among others.

Visually exciting, emotionally powerful, this is imaginative theatre with a capital "T." Suitable for arena staging. Highly recommended for *all* groups -- high school, college, amateur, professional.

ABOUT THE SETTING

The basic set is the open stage. A few simple props suggest various locations. Some of these props are positioned prior to the beginning of each act; others are carried on and off by the actors. The "stage picture" should resemble a film. Play should not be presented as a series of "scenes," but as a continuous flow of action, one scene blending into the next. No waits, no pauses. Avoid fragmentation and choppiness. For the purpose of rehearsals, however, individual scenes and locales have been indicated. For additional staging suggestions, consult PRODUCTION NOTES.

ACT ONE

Prologue

SCENE: *Entire Company is onstage, silhouetted in dim lighting. The ACTORS are like shadows. A moment passes and VICTOR H., the author, enters DR. He stands in a shaft of light that separates him from the others. He address the audience.*

VICTOR H. My name is Victor Hugo. *(Pause.)* I am a writer. *(Indicates ACTORS.)* These actors are my creations. For you, they will act out a story of great sadness and some joy. Isn't that what life is about? Sadness and joy? *(Briskly.)* You will meet them all. Fantine, Cosette, Marius, Inspector Javert and, of course, Jean Valjean. And you will meet -- others.

THENARDIER *(calling into audience).* Thenardier!

MME. THENARDIER. Madame Thenardier!

EPONINE. Eponine!

AZELMA. Azelma!

CHAMPMATHIEU. Champmathieu! Prisoner of the State!

VICTOR H. Ah, yes. "Prisoner of the State." That has a familiar ring.

EPONINE. Give us something to eat, Monsieur. We are hungry.

THENARDIER. Give us something to steal, Monsieur. We are thieves! *(Laughter.)*

VICTOR H *(when laughter subsides).* Laughter not from the heart, but from the empty belly. Laughter that mocks itself. *(A step forward, a gesture to the others.)* There is a point at which the unfortunate and the infamous are associated and confounded in a single word, a *fatal* word -- "Les Misérables." *(Like a circus ringmaster, he claps his hands and the "shadows" exit L and R. To audience.)* The sickness of a nation does not kill Man. To doctor is to do a great deal; to enlighten is to do still more. Nevertheless, those of us who study the health of society must now and again shake our heads. *(Gestures to the*

7

open stage space.) Our canvas is one of imagination. *(Briskly.)* The month is October. A man traveling on foot has entered the town.

(JEAN VALJEAN enters forestage from DL. Shabbily dressed and dirty-looking. Over one shoulder he carries a sack. As VICTOR H. speaks, VALJEAN takes a step toward him, stops.)

VICTOR H. No one knew him. No one wanted to know him. Why should they?

VALJEAN *(muttering).* Why should they, indeed... why should anyone want to know me...?

VICTOR H. His name -- Jean Valjean. Recently freed from prison. His term -- nineteen years. His crime -- stealing a loaf of bread to feed his widowed sister and her large family.

(VICTOR H. exits R on forestage and general stage lighting dims up somewhat. At this point we can see some stage properties. Table and chairs, or stools, C. On the table are a pair of silver candlesticks. SR there is a bench. SL there is another bench, only this one is wide enough to later suggest a bed or cot.)

SCENE ONE

SCENE: *Town street, forestage. Night. Still muttering to himself, VALJEAN puts his sack on the ground and kneels beside it. He "pokes" at it as one might "fluff" a pillow. He stretches out, his head on the sack. Ready for sleep.*

VALJEAN. "Where am I to go?" That's what I always ask. "Somewhere else." That's what they always answer. "Somewhere else." Where do I find this land of "Somewhere Else?"

(MME. MAGLIORE, a citizen of the town, enters from DL, reacts to the sight of the tramp.)

MME. MAGLIORE. What are you doing?

VALJEAN. Eh?

MME. MAGLIORE. I said -- what are you doing? *(VALJEAN opens his eyes, sits up.)*

VALJEAN. My good woman, you can see what I'm doing. I'm sleeping here. Or *trying* to.

MME. MAGLIORE. On the ground?

VALJEAN. For nineteen years I slept on a wooden mattress. What difference does it make?

MME. MAGLIORE. Were you a soldier?

VALJEAN *(lies)*. Yes. A soldier. What is the name of this town?

MME. MAGLIORE. Digne.

VALJEAN. To me, one town looks like another.

MME. MAGLIORE. Why don't you go to an inn?

VALJEAN *(lies)*. I have no money.

MME. MAGLIORE. Alas, I have only four sous in my pocket.

VALJEAN *(gets to his feet)*. That's better than nothing. *(MME. MAGLIORE takes the coins from some pocket. Holds them out. Greedily, VALJEAN snatches them away and into his own pocket.)*

MME. MAGLIORE. Four sous won't pay for lodging at an inn. You can't possibly spend the night here on the ground. You must be cold and hungry.

VALJEAN. I'm no stranger to cold and hunger.

MME. MAGLIORE. Surely, someone will take you in out of charity.

VALJEAN. I've knocked at every door. I've been turned away everywhere. *(MME. MAGLIORE points in the direction of the table with the candlesticks.)*

MME. MAGLIORE. Have you knocked at that house?

VALJEAN. No.

MME. MAGLIORE. Then do. *(Points L.)* Around the little path. You'll find the door. *(VALJEAN doesn't move.)* Go on. Do as I say. *(MME. MAGLIORE exits DR. VALJEAN looks after her, deciding whether or not to take her advice.)*

VALJEAN. Why not? What's one more door slammed in my face? *(He picks up his sack and tosses it over his shoulder, exits DL.)*

SCENE TWO

SCENE: *Cottage of MONSEIGNEUR MYRIEL, Bishop of the town. Night. MONSEIGNEUR MYRIEL enters from SR. He wears a cleric's cap. He carries a book of prayers and as he walks to the table his talkative sister, MLLE. BAPTISTINE, dogs his steps.*

MLLE. BAPTISTINE. Everyone's talking about it. I don't understand why you haven't heard. You know everything that transpires in this town. And why shouldn't you? (*MONSEIGNEUR MYRIEL closes his book of prayers, sits.*)

MONSEIGNEUR MYRIEL. I see my prayers will have to wait. (*Puts book on table.*) What are you talking about?

MLLE. BAPTISTINE. There's a dangerous beggar in town. He's been seen.

MONSEIGNEUR MYRIEL. Is being seen a crime?

MLLE. BAPTISTINE. Probably a gypsy. He goes from house to house trying to get lodging. They say he has a terrible look on his face.

MONSEIGNEUR MYRIEL (*amused*). A *terrible* look? My, my.

MLLE. BAPTISTINE. Something dreadful will happen tonight, everyone says so.

MONSEIGNEUR MYRIEL. If everyone says so, it must be true.

MLLE. BAPTISTINE. You think I'm silly. We need bolts on the door. Any stranger can walk in.

(*VALJEAN enters from SL and approaches the cottage. Stands outside as MLLE. BAPTISTINE rambles on.*)

MLLE. BAPTISTINE. A town buried in the mountains like this one with not a single lantern in the streets. (*She breaks off as she sees VALJEAN standing in the "open doorway." Stifles a scream, points.*) The gypsy. (*MONSEIGNEUR MYRIEL turns, stands.*)

VALJEAN. I mean no harm to anyone.

MONSEIGNEUR MYRIEL. You are welcome in my house.

MLLE. BAPTISTINE *(sotto)*. Madness. *(VALJEAN speaks directly.)*

VALJEAN. Look. My name is Jean Valjean. I'm a convict on parole.

MLLE. BAPTISTINE. Auugh. There, Brother, what did I tell you!?

MONSEIGNEUR MYRIEL. Be quiet, Baptistine. *(She pouts.)* Go on.

VALJEAN. They let me out four days ago and I've barely eaten since. I am walking to Pontarlier.

MONSEIGNEUR MYRIEL. That is a great distance. *(To MLLE. BAPTISTINE.)* Bring some food for our guest.

MLLE. BAPTISTINE. Guest?! *(MLLE. BAPTISTINE tosses up her hands in despair, exits R. MONSEIGNEUR MYRIEL motions to VALJEAN.)*

MONSEIGNEUR MYRIEL. Come in, come in, my son. *(Warily, like a hunted animal, VALJEAN moves closer to the table. His eyes darting about.)*

VALJEAN. When I came to this town I went to an inn. They turned me out. I had to show them my prison papers. It's the law.

MONSEIGNEUR MYRIEL. I know.

VALJEAN. If I don't show my papers they can send me back.

MONSEIGNEUR MYRIEL. No papers are required here. *(Glad for the opportunity to talk openly with someone who appears sympathetic, VALJEAN pours out his woe.)*

VALJEAN. I tried another inn and the woman told me to clear out. I tried the jail and the doorkeeper wouldn't open. I crawled into a dog kennel and the dog drove me out just as if he were a man and knew who I was. I can't wash away the stink of prison. I thought I'd sleep in a field under the stars, but there weren't any stars and it looked as though it was going to rain. I lay down in the street and a good woman pointed to this cottage and said I should try here.

MONSEIGNEUR MYRIEL. She did right.

(MLLE. BAPTISTINE returns, still nervous about the visitor. In one hand she has a bowl with a spoon sticking out. In the

other hand, she carries a small loaf of bread or a roll. With an air of defiance, she puts the meal on the table and starts to exit.)

MONSEIGNEUR MYRIEL. Baptistine.

MLLE. BAPTISTINE *(sharp)*. What is it? *(She turns.)*

MONSEIGNEUR MYRIEL. You've forgotten the wine.

MLLE. BAPTISTINE. His sort is used to water.

MONSEIGNEUR MYRIEL *(gently)*. A glass of wine for our guest. *(Reluctantly, she nods, exits.)* Forgive my sister. Kindness, I fear, is not one of her virtues. *(Gestures that VALJEAN should sit.)* Please. *(VALJEAN drops his sack, sits at the table and attacks his food. His eyes continue to dart about -- as if he feared some enemy might materialize and snatch away his bread and soup.)*

VALJEAN. I didn't tell the good woman I was an ex-convict. She thought I was a soldier. She gave me four sous. But I have money. The money I earned by nineteen years' work in prison.

(MLLE. BAPTISTINE enters with a glass of wine.)

MONSEIGNEUR MYRIEL. Here's your wine. *(He takes the glass from MLLE. BAPTISTINE.)* Thank you, Baptistine. *(MLLE. BAPTISTINE gives them both a look of disapproval, exits. MONSEIGNEUR MYRIEL puts the wine in front of VALJEAN. He grabs the glass and drains it in thirsty gulps, slams the glass back to the table.)*

VALJEAN *(gobbling the bread, slurping the soup)*. What is this place? Is it an inn? I'm ready to pay. I don't care how much. I'm very tired. Will you let me stay? I've walked I don't know how many leagues.

MONSEIGNEUR MYRIEL. You are welcome to stay, Monsieur Valjean.

VALJEAN. *Monsieur*? You call *me* monsieur? *(Annoyed.)* Weren't you listening? I'm a convict. *(Reaches inside his clothing and pulls out some yellow papers.)* This is my parole. Read it: "Five years for robbery with violence. Fourteen years for four attempts to escape -- a very dangerous man." Look, I'll

show you. *(Rolls up his sleeve, indicates a spot on his arm.)*
That tattoo marks me. Convict, convict. *Convict.*

MONSEIGNEUR MYRIEL. I've seen such markings before.

VALJEAN. So there you are. Will you turn me out? Or, will
you give me a bed for the night? Do you have a stable or a
barn?

MONSEIGNEUR MYRIEL. There is a room with a bed. It is
yours.

VALJEAN. You mean it? You won't throw me out? *(MON-
SEIGNEUR MYRIEL smiles, shakes his head.)* You're a good
man. *(Yawns.)* You're an innkeeper, aren't you?

MONSEIGNEUR MYRIEL. I am a priest and this is where I
live.

VALJEAN. A priest! But of course. I'm stupid. I didn't notice
your cleric's cap. You're human, Monsieur le Cure. You
don't despise people. *(He yawns again.)* Forgive me. I can't
keep my eyes open. *(MONSEIGNEUR MYRIEL takes a
match which is by one of the candles, strikes it.)*

MONSEIGNEUR MYRIEL. Then you must sleep. *(Lights a
candle.)* You've suffered a great deal.

VALJEAN. But I've learned things. There are classes in prison
for anyone who wants to learn. *(Laughs self-mockingly.)*
That's where I learned to read and write. I'm a clever fellow
underneath this dirt.

MONSEIGNEUR MYRIEL. This candle will light your way.
You'll find the room. *(Indicates the bench - cot - SL.)* There.
(VALJEAN takes the candle, stands.)

VALJEAN. The candlestick is heavy.

MONSEIGNEUR MYRIEL. It's silver.

VALJEAN. Silver? *Real* silver? I'm not used to such luxury.

MONSEIGNEUR MYRIEL. Sleep well, Jean Valjean. Before
you leave tomorrow you must have a bowl of warm milk from
our cows.

VALJEAN. *Fresh* warm milk? It's been a long time. Thank you,
Father. *(Candlestick in hand, VALJEAN picks up his sack,
crosses to his "room." He sits on the edge of the cot. Blows out
the candle flame, sets the sack and candlestick on the floor. Ex-
hausted, he falls back on the cot, sleeps.)*

(While this bit of pantomime plays, MLLE. BAPTISTINE returns. Picks up bowl and wine glass.)

MLLE. BAPTISTINE. He didn't finish the soup.

MONSEIGNEUR MYRIEL. Sleep is what he needs.

MLLE. BAPTISTINE. You are my brother and you are a bishop, but sometimes my brother and the bishop are both fools.

MONSEIGNEUR MYRIEL. Even fools have their place.

MLLE. BAPTISTINE. Have you thought what you're doing? How do you know he's never murdered anyone?

MONSEIGNEUR MYRIEL. That is God's affair.

MLLE. BAPTISTINE *(as she exits)*. I'll say nothing further. *(Touch of sarcasm.)* After all, what do I understand of the world? I am only one woman in a small town. Whatever my brother does is right. Whatever the bishop says is true. *(She's out.)*

MONSEIGNEUR MYRIEL *(calls after her)*. I am pleased you had nothing further to say, Baptistine. *(Looks to VALJEAN's room.)* Nineteen long years. *(He follows after MLLE. BAPTISTINE and the lights dim down to indicate a passage of time. Moments pass. Slowly, VALJEAN sits up. He listens. He gets out of bed, listens again. Satisfied it's "all clear," he drops to his knees and seizes the candlestick. His criminal instincts are in full bloom.)*

VALJEAN. Silver. Solid silver. I can feel the weight. *(Gleeful.)* And the worth. *(Without a second's hesitation, he thrusts the candlestick into the sack, stands and creeps off, SL. More moments pass to indicate the approach of morning.)*

(MLLE. BAPTISTINE enters from R, straightening her dress. She's just come from her room and is yawning. Suddenly, she remembers VALJEAN.)

MLLE. BAPTISTINE. It's after sunup. Time that gypsy was on his way. *(With a purposeful stride she walks to the "bedroom," stand outside, calls.)* Monsieur? Monsieur, the sun is up. Time for you to go. *(Listens.)* Monsieur, answer me. *(Enters room. At once she realizes the ex-convict has fled.)* Gone!

(Searches.) And the candlestick with him. Thief! *(She runs back to the table and checks to see if the other candlestick is still there. She yells off-stage R.)* See what your charity has done. Oh, you foolish man! So gullible!

(MONSEIGNEUR MYRIEL enters, R.)

MONSEIGNEUR MYRIEL. Calm yourself, Baptistine.

MLLE. BAPTISTINE. Calm myself, calm myself. Is that all you can say? It's a miracle he didn't cut our throats. He's gone!

MONSEIGNEUR MYRIEL. So, then, he's gone. There's no need to carry on in this manner. He probably wanted an early start.

MLLE. BAPTISTINE. He's stolen from you! *(Points to remaining candlestick.)* There's only one left. He's stolen the silver candlestick you lighted for him. Who knows what else?

(Three MEN enter from SL. Two are POLICEMEN, a sergeant and a lower rank. Between them, head bowed, is VALJEAN. The POLICEMAN holds the sack. They stand in the open "doorway.")

SERGEANT. Monseigneur.

MLLE. BAPTISTINE. They've got him. What good luck. *(SERGEANT shoves VALJEAN into the cottage.)*

MONSEIGNEUR MYRIEL. So here you are, Jean! I'm delighted to see you again. You forgot the other candlestick. What good is only one candlestick when it belongs to a pair?

MLLE. BAPTISTINE. What are you saying?

SERGEANT *(surprised)*. Monseigneur, when we saw him he seemed to be on the run. We wanted to make sure. *(Reaches into sack and takes out the other candlestick.)* We found this in his knapsack.

MLLE. BAPTISTINE. I knew it.

MONSEIGNEUR MYRIEL. And he told you the priest had given it to him. I can see how it was. You felt bound to bring him here. But you are mistaken.

SERGEANT. You mean we can let him go?

MONSEIGNEUR MYRIEL. Certainly.

VALJEAN *(slowly lifts his head)*. Am I really allowed to go?

SERGEANT. You heard. *(With a nod, SERGEANT indicates POLICEMAN should return the sack to VALJEAN. He does, along with the candlestick, which he drops inside.)*

MONSEIGNEUR MYRIEL. Thank you, gentlemen.

SERGEANT *(salutes)*. Monseigneur. *(He nods to MLLE. BAPTISTINE, exits L. POLICEMAN follows. VALJEAN looks hopeless and helpless. He's trembling.)*

MLLE. BAPTISTINE. Mad. That's what you are -- mad. *(On the verge of tears, she runs off, R.)*

VALJEAN. You could have sent me back to prison. Back to the stink and the pain. *(Mystified by MONSEIGNEUR MYRIEL's action.)* Why -- ?

MONSEIGNEUR MYRIEL. Sell the candlesticks. Use the money to make yourself an honest man.

VALJEAN. I had forgotten what it was like to feel shame. *(Impulsively, he drops to one knee and clutches MONSEIGNEUR MYRIEL's hand.)* Forgive me.

MONSEIGNEUR MYRIEL *(helps him up)*. It is time for you to forgive yourself. And the world if you can. Promise you will do as I asked?

VALJEAN (deeply felt). Yes.

MONSEIGNEUR MYRIEL. Always remember, you no longer belong to what is evil but to what is good. *(He hands him the table candlestick.)* Now, Jean, go in peace. The door here is never locked. *(VALJEAN stares at MONSEIGNEUR MYRIEL a moment. Words are useless. Clutching the table candlestick and the sack, he leaves the cottage and exits up SL. The lighting shifts and MONSEIGNEUR MYRIEL slowly walks off-stage in the same direction VALJEAN has taken. MONSEIGNEUR MYRIEL is lost in his thoughts.)*

SCENE THREE

SCENE: *Outside the Thenardier Inn. Day. The exterior of the inn is represented by the bench placed SR. As MONSEIGNEUR MYRIEL moves to exit, the POLICEMEN return - or*

STAGEHANDS wearing blue smocks to suggest workmen of the period - and move the table upstage and position it at an angle. Table now becomes a "multi- purpose" prop. When this is done they exit. As MONSEIGNEUR MYRIEL exits and the POLICEMEN reposition the table, MME. THENARDIER enters R carrying a bowl of potatoes and a knife. She sits, placing the bowl on the ground. She begins to peel.

THENARDIER's VOICE *(from off-stage)*. Louise!
MME. THENARDIER. I'm here.
THENARDIER's VOICE. I must see you.
MME. THENARDIER. Come outside.

(She continues her work. Her husband, THENARDIER, a gruff, evil individual enters behind her. He holds some papers.)

THENARDIER *(slaps at the papers)*. How am I to pay these new bills?
MME. THENARDIER *(calmly)*. Is it my fault you put too much water in the wine and customers stay away?
THENARDIER. That's no way for a wife to speak.
MME. THENARDIER. Wife? I'm more of a workhorse. *(He makes as if to strike her.)*
THENARDIER. Mind your mouth, or I'll shut it.
MME. THENARDIER. You're good at that.
THENARDIER *(the papers)*. I won't pay! They're trying to cheat me.

(From DL on the forestage enters FANTINE. She's a pretty, young girl. Vulnerable. She carries an infant - doll - wrapped in a blanket. Holds a traveling or carpetbag. She makes her way toward the inn.)

MME. THENARDIER. If you don't pay they won't make deliveries. If they won't make deliveries, we might as well close up.
THENARDIER. They pad these bills. Besides, I don't water the wine. I spit in it. *(He laughs, exits. MME. THENARDIER notices FANTINE.)*

MME. THENARDIER. Good day.

FANTINE. Good day, Madame. Is this the road to Paris?

MME. THENARDIER. It is. That your child?

FANTINE. Yes. *(MME. THENARDIER stands, moves to get a closer look.)*

MME. THENARDIER. I'm fond of children. I have two of my own. Both baby girls. *(Looks at infant.)* A pretty thing. Boy or girl?

FANTINE. It's a girl. Cosette.

MME. THENARDIER. May I hold her?

FANTINE. Of course. *(MME. THENARDIER takes the infant, rocks it in her arms.)*

MME. THENARDIER. My name is Thenardier. My husband and I keep this inn. It's not easy, I don't mind telling you.

FANTINE. It's a lovely spot, Madame. The air is so clean. The country is a good place for children.

MME. THENARDIER. None better. My babies are Eponine and Azelma. Cosette. Eponine and Azelma -- they might be sisters.

FANTINE. Yes. *(Quickly.)* Madame -- will you look after my daughter for me?

MME. THENARDIER. What -- ?

FANTINE. I can't take her with me where I'm going. I have to find work and it's not easy if you have a child. You have girls of your own. As you say, they would be like sisters. She'd be no trouble. She never cries. No one's taught her to smile, but she smiles all the time. She's a happy baby.

MME. THENARDIER *(suddenly cold)*. How much could you pay?

FANTINE *(a moment's hesitation)*. I could pay six francs a month.

THENARDIER's VOICE *(from inside inn)*. Seven!

(THENARDIER comes into view. It's plain he's been eavesdropping.)

THENARDIER. Not less than seven, and six months in advance.

MME. THENARDIER *(to FANTINE)*. My husband.

FANTINE *(curtsies)*. Monsieur.

THENARDIER. Six times seven makes forty-two.

MME. THENARDIER. And another fifteen francs for extras. There are always extra expenses with a baby.

THENARDIER. Total, fifty-seven francs. Can you pay that?

FANTINE. I have eighty francs. I'll have enough to get to Paris if I go on foot. I'll find work there and when I've saved a little, I'll come for her.

THENARDIER. Has she enough clothes?

MME. THENARDIER. You can't expect us to take on that expense.

FANTINE *(holds up bag)*. She has a beautiful little wardrobe. Here in the bag.

THENARDIER. Very well then. Come inside. We'll settle matters over a glass of wine.

FANTINE *(to MME. THENARDIER)*. Let me have her.

MME. THENARDIER *(passes INFANT to FANTINE)*. Don't worry about a thing. I'll take good care of her. *(FANTINE forces a smile. THENARDIER motions to the inn and FANTINE and BABY enter. When she's out of earshot -- .)*

THENARDIER. Seven a month. Not bad.

MME. THENARDIER. If she makes the payments.

THENARDIER. She'd better. Otherwise, the brat goes into the river.

MME. THENARDIER. The baby clothes ought to fetch a fair price. I'll sell them tomorrow.

THENARDIER. Did she mention a husband?

MME. THENARDIER. Do they ever? *(THENARDIER shrugs, goes into inn. MME. THENARDIER picks up the bowl, follows after.)*

SCENE FOUR

SCENE: *A factory yard in the town of Montfermeil. It is a few years later. Day. MME. VICTURNIEN, a dour woman in charge of the employees, enters from UL. She is ringing a hand bell.*

MME. VICTURNIEN. Lunch! Time for lunch! *(More bell ringing.)* Lunch! Time for lunch! Hurry along.

(FAUCHELEVENT, a vendor, enters DL. Over one shoulder he carries a straw basket which contains bread, rolls and a bottle of wine. Some tin cups are attached to the basket. As MME. VICTURNIEN and FAUCHELEVENT converse, three factory GIRLS enter, R and L. NOTE: EXTRAS can be added. GIRLS sit on the stools and bench - and the cot if more space is needed.)

FAUCHELEVENT. I bid you good day, Mme. Victurnien.

MME. VICTURNIEN. Good day, Fauchelevent.

FAUCHELEVENT. And how is our benefactor today?

MME. VICTURNIEN. Monsieur Madeleine is away on business.

FAUCHELEVENT. Business, always business. A remarkable man. *(FAUCHELEVENT moves from worker to worker. When they hand him a coin, he gives them bread and a cup. Into the cup he pours wine.)*

GIRL #3. Remarkable enough to bring this town to life. We'd all be starving if it weren't for Monsieur Madeleine.

GIRL #1. He's a saint.

FAUCHELEVENT. And don't I know it. Thanks to him I can walk. My back isn't broken. You recall, Mme. Victurnien, I was caught under the wheels on my own cart.

MME. VICTURNIEN *(bored, it's a story she's heard many times.)* Yes, yes.

FAUCHELEVENT *(to GIRLS).* I would have died, but for Monsieur Madeleine. Our good mayor has the strength of an ox. The police tried to help but they couldn't. But our mayor slipped under the cart and pushed with his shoulders until there was room enough to pull me out.

MME. VICTURNIEN. You talk as if nothing happened in your life before Monsieur Madeleine saved you.

FAUCHELEVENT. That is the way I feel.

GIRL #1. More wine, Fauchelevent. *(He pours more wine into her cup.)*

FAUCHELEVENT. He's given us the school and the hospital. God bless Monsieur Madeleine.

OTHERS. God bless Monsieur Madeleine.

GIRL #2. The best part is he has no wife -- yet. *(GIRLS giggle.)*

MME. VICTURNIEN. Be still, girls. Monsieur Madeleine is wedded to his work.

FAUCHELEVENT. We're all better off for it.

GIRL #3. Anyway, saints don't marry. *(More giggles.)*

(FANTINE enters from R. Much older in appearance than when we first met her. Tired. She fights hard to conceal a troublesome cough. Sits. FAUCHELEVENT crosses to her, but FANTINE shakes her head and FAUCHELEVENT moves off, exits.)

GIRL #1. The girl from "Paris" is not hungry today.

GIRL #2. She never wants to eat.

GIRL #3. Too good "to dine" with the likes of us.

GIRL #1. She's used to Paris restaurants. *(GIRLS laugh. FANTINE does her best to ignore them. Coughs. GIRL #1 jumps up.)* There, Madame, she's doing it again. She has the cough. She'll infect us all.

FANTINE. No, no, please. It's only a little cough. I must have caught a chill.

GIRL #2. She coughs all the time. Her handkerchief has spots of blood. I've seen them. Why should we work beside her and risk consumption?

GIRL #3. Besides, she's not a good worker, Mme. Victurnien. Too slow.

FANTINE *(suddenly alarmed)*. I work as fast as anyone. Faster. I string twenty necklaces of black beads in an hour. And the necklaces are always perfect.

GIRL #1. She has a child, Mme. Victurnien. It's town gossip. A child, but no husband. That's what they say.

FANTINE *(to her feet)*. That's not true.

MME. VICTURNIEN. I'll attend to this. *(To GIRL #1.)* It's none of your concern. Leave "Mademoiselle" Fantine to me.

GIRL #2. Another "Mademoiselle" from Paris. They're all the same.

GIRL #3. Thinking they're better than everyone else.

GIRL #1. Always like some shy, fine lady, instead of a factory worker.

MME. VICTURNIEN. Enough of that. Go along, all of you. *(Sensing FANTINE is about to be discharged, GIRLS slowly exit -- grins on their faces.)*

FANTINE. Please, Mme. Victurnien, don't listen to gossip.

MME. VICTURNIEN. I do not like liars, and you are a liar, Mademoiselle. You do have a child. Your letters to Mme. Thenardier have aroused the curiosity of the town. It is my duty to see that this factory harbors nothing that would bring discredit on Monsieur Madeleine.

FANTINE. Let me speak with Monsieur Madeleine.

MME. VICTURNIEN. He is away. In his absence I am in complete charge of this factory. I took it upon myself to visit the inn run by Mme. Thenardier and her husband. I have seen the nasty little girl. *(FANTINE burns with anger and we see a new side to her personality. She is like a mother tigress protecting her cub.)*

FANTINE. You wicked, wicked busybody! You're hateful!

MME. VICTURNIEN. How dare you!

FANTINE *(suddenly contrite)*. I'm sorry. I didn't mean that. *(Frantic.)* Madame, please. You can't discharge me. My daughter's board costs me ten sous a day and I make only twelve. I have debts.

MME. VICTURNIEN. You are a shameful young woman, Mademoiselle. I have my duty. You will leave this factory -- now.

FANTINE. No! Mme. Victurnien, I am *begging.* Not for myself. For my child. Let me stay. Let me work. I'll work harder than before. I'll work for less money. I'll manage somehow. I'll survive.

MME. VICTURNIEN. Your sort always does. Be off these premises in five minutes, or I shall send for the police.

FANTINE *(horrified)*. The police?!

MME. VICTURNIEN *(rings the hand bell, exits R.)* To work! To work! *(FANTINE is crushed.)*

FANTINE. Cosette... my poor, poor Cosette. *(With a sigh of resignation, FANTINE exits L.)*

SCENE FIVE

SCENE: *Outside the Thenardier Inn. THENARDIER comes from the inn with a bucket. He pantomimes tossing out some water. As he does this, MME. THENARDIER, with market basket, waving a letter, enters on forestage, from L.*

MME. THENARDIER. A letter! She's sent us another letter.

THENARDIER. What good's a letter to you? You can't read. You're too thick between the ears. I'm the scholar. Give it here.

MME. THENARDIER. Where is it from? *(He takes the letter, squints at the postmark.)*

THENARDIER. The town of Montfermeil. She's still there.

MME. THENARDIER. I liked it better when her letters came from Paris.

THENARDIER. What difference does it make -- as long as there's money inside.

MME. THENARDIER. I've always wanted to go to Paris. There's money to be made there. *(He rips open the envelope, takes out a letter, checks for money. He shakes the envelope.)*

THENARDIER. Not a sou.

MME. THENARDIER. What does she say?

THENARDIER. Let's see. *(Scans the letter.)* Hmmmmm. She's lost her job.

MME. THENARDIER. What bad luck. You see, she was better off in Paris.

THENARDIER. Not for us, she wasn't. She made more money in Montfermeil. I know how to milk a cow. I'll write to her.

MME. THENARDIER. What are you going to say?

THENARDIER. I'll say Cosette is ill. We need forty francs for the doctor.

MME. THENARDIER. But she says she's lost her job.

THENARDIER. If she thinks her brat is down with the fever she'll find work fast enough.

MME. THENARDIER. Don't say fever. We used that last year to get twenty-five francs out of her. It won't work a second time.

THENARDIER. I'll think of something. Leave it to me.

MME. THENARDIER. You're crafty as a fox.

THENARDIER *(confirms)*. True enough.

MME. THENARDIER. Heaven pity us hens. *(MME. THENAR-DIER enters the inn. THENARDIER, studying the letter, follows.)*

SCENE SIX

SCENE: *A street - forestage. Night. MARGUERITE, a young girl, enters DL and moves C. She carries a tray of flowers.*

MARGUERITE. Flowers... I have flowers...

(From DR enter a young MAN and WOMAN. MARGUERITE moves to them.)

MARGUERITE. Flowers? Flowers for your young lady, monsieur? *(He shakes his head. Young MAN and WOMAN exit DL.)*

(INSPECTOR JAVERT, in charge of the local police, enters from DR. MARGUERITE stiffens when she sees him, starts to follow after the young MAN and WOMAN.)

JAVERT. You there. Stop. *(MARGUERITE sighs, stops. Turns to JAVERT. The police official is an exacting man. He never smiles. The letter of the law is his religion.)*

MARGUERITE *(forces a smile)*. Good evening, Inspector Javert.

JAVERT. Your name?

MARGUERITE. Marguerite Robillard.

JAVERT *(no nonsense)*. Let me see your license.

MARGUERITE *(dutifully)*. Yes, Inspector. *(She produces a license, hands it to JAVERT. He checks it.)*

JAVERT. This license expires in two days' time, Mademoiselle Robillard.

MARGUERITE. Yes.

JAVERT. You know the law. You can't sell without a license. See that you have this renewed.

MARGUERITE. I won't forget.

JAVERT. I assure you I will not. The fine is thirty-five francs for the first offense. Second offense will mean seven days in jail.

MARGUERITE *(nervously)*. In two days -- a new license.

JAVERT. I trust so -- for your sake. *(JAVERT returns the license, walks off, DL. MARGUERITE makes a face after him, sticks out her tongue.)*

MARGUERITE. Awful man.

(FANTINE, a ragged shawl over her shoulders, enters from DR. She holds a hand to her cheek, head down. MARGUERITE steps to her.)

MARGUERITE. Fantine. *(FANTINE looks up.)*

FANTINE. Oh. Marguerite.

MARGUERITE. The landlady has locked you out again. Climb up the back stairs and into my room. Don't let her see you. If she does, she'll toss me out, too.

FANTINE. I have money. *(Opens her fist to show a couple of coins.)*

MARGUERITE *(amazed)*. Two Napoleons! Where did you get them? *(Quick, FANTINE opens her mouth and stretches back her lips.)*

FANTINE. My back teeth.

MARGUERITE *(horrified)*. What are you saying?

FANTINE. The dentist said I had fine molars. He sells sets of false teeth to those who can pay his price.

MARGUERITE. How horrible. The monster! I'd sooner throw myself out of a top-story window. It's a crime such men are allowed to practice. Hair grows back but not teeth. What could you have been thinking of?

FANTINE. What difference does it make? One week I sell my hair, the next my teeth. God is forgetting me piece by piece.

MARGUERITE. Oh, Fantine. *(Sighs.)* At least you can pay the landlady. *(FANTINE coughs.)*

FANTINE. Not a sou, no.

MARGUERITE. That cough doesn't get any better. Use a few francs. See a doctor. Buy some medicine.

FANTINE. The money is for Cosette.

MARGUERITE. Cosette, Cosette. Always Cosette. You never think of yourself. *(Shrugs.)* Do as you must. But, remember, be quiet when you creep up the back stairs.

FANTINE. You are a good friend, Marguerite.

MARGUERITE. I do what I can. *(Moves off, DL.)* Flowers... I have flowers... flowers... *(FANTINE takes a hanky from her pocket and dabs inside her mouth.)*

(BAMATABOIS, a young man of the town, an idler, strolls into view from DR. He watches FANTINE for a moment, grins. He circles about her. FANTINE gives him a cold look.)

FANTINE. What are you looking at?

BAMATABOIS. I've seen you before. You used to be quite pretty. What a sight -- catching you in the dentist's window having your teeth pulled. Some show.

FANTINE *(hard)*. I don't know you. I don't want to know you. Go away.

BAMATABOIS. Must have hurt something wicked. Let me have a look. *(He goes to touch her mouth. She slaps his hand away.)*

FANTINE. I'm not an animal.

BAMATABOIS. Temper, temper.

FANTINE. Leave me alone. I'm warning you.

BAMATABOIS *(enjoys tormenting her)*. You? Warning me? That's a laugh. Anyone would think you were a rich lady with a fine house. *(FANTINE turns her back on him, starts to walk away.)*

FANTINE. Go to the devil. *(Gleeful, BAMATABOIS steps after her and tears away the pitiful shawl.)*

BAMATABOIS *(waving the shawl about)*. Look what I've got, look what I've got! *(In a fury, FANTINE spins around.)*

FANTINE. Give it back!

BAMATABOIS. Ha, ha. Ha, ha! *(Deliberately, he tears it in two.)*

FANTINE. You miserable man!

(As she berates him, she strikes at him with her fists. Attracted by the commotion, young MAN and WOMAN return, stand DL, watching. BAMATABOIS shoves FANTINE to the ground.)

BAMATABOIS. Don't hit me, you toothless witch! *(More furious than before, FANTINE springs to her feet and continues to strike at BAMATABOIS.)*

FANTINE. You're right! I'm a witch and I'll prove it! *(Another fist to his face.)*

BAMATABOIS. That's enough. Stop! People are looking.

FANTINE. Let them! *(She grabs BAMATABOIS by the hair and pulls.)*

BAMATABOIS. Auuuuuugh!

(JAVERT enters DL, pushes between the young MAN and WOMAN, crosses to FANTINE and pulls her away from the still protesting BAMATABOIS.)

BAMATABOIS. Auuuuuuuugh!

JAVERT. Enough of that!

FANTINE. He started it!

BAMATABOIS. I did not. She did.

JAVERT *(to onlookers)*. This is police business. *(On hearing "police," FANTINE calms down, recognizes JAVERT. Young MAN and WOMAN exit.)*

FANTINE. It wasn't my fault.

JAVERT *(to BAMATABOIS)*. You. What are you waiting for? Do you want me to run you in? Get out of here.

BAMATABOIS. Yes, sir. *(He hurries out, DL. Drops shawl.)*

JAVERT. You come along with me. Move.

FANTINE. That's my shawl. *(She picks it up, sees it torn beyond repair.)* What's the use?

JAVERT. You heard me. Move.

FANTINE *(worried)*. Where are we going?

JAVERT. Where do you think? You'll get six months for this. I'll see to it.

FANTINE. But it wasn't my fault, I tell you!

JAVERT. Don't make it any worse than it already is. *(He shoves her R.)*

FANTINE. Six months?

JAVERT. Six months in prison. The law's the law. *(Another shove and they're out.)*

SCENE SEVEN

SCENE: *Police Headquarters -- represented by the table. POLICEMAN enters from L. He has an envelope in his hand. He steps to the table, studies the handwriting on the envelope for a moment. Puts it down. Next, he places a stool behind the table, sits. Glad for a moment of quiet, he takes out a small, clay pipe, prepares to smoke. Voices from off-stage R.*

FANTINE's VOICE. Monsieur Javert, I beg you to be merciful. It was not my fault. If you had seen how it started you would know.

JAVERT. Be quiet. *(On hearing JAVERT's VOICE, POLICEMAN jumps up, pockets pipe. Stands at attention.)*

(JAVERT enters. He holds FANTINE by the arm.)

POLICEMAN *(indicates letter)*. On your desk, Inspector. It's marked "urgent."

FANTINE. Six months. Six months in prison, earning seven sous a day! A fine of four sous if I drop a stitch. What about my daughter? What right had that man to torment me? *(As she pleads, JAVERT goes behind the table, sits. He opens the letter, reads the contents.)* Let me off just this once, Monsieur Javert. I'll never again be any trouble.

JAVERT *(a command)*. Sit down. *(FANTINE sits, terrified by the turn of events. POLICEMAN stands at attention, JAVERT continues to read. FANTINE can't control herself. Again, she starts to plead.)*

FANTINE. I'm not very well, you see. And when he began to mock me, I lost my temper. Is there no one who saw what happened and can tell you? *(Troubled by the contents of the letter, JAVERT crumples the paper in his fist, puts it aside.)*

JAVERT. You're getting six months and not even the Archbishop of Paris can alter that.

FANTINE. Mercy. Have pity. *(JAVERT nods to POLICEMAN. He moves to FANTINE, who drops to her knees.)* Pity. If not for me, for my child.

POLICEMAN. Come on, you. Get up. *(He pulls a sobbing FANTINE to her feet.)*

JAVERT. Take her away.

FANTINE. *No!*

(VALJEAN enters R.)

VALJEAN. One moment, if you please.

JAVERT *(stands, surprised)*. Monsieur Mayor. *(The mayor, Monsieur Madeleine, is the man we first met as JEAN VALJEAN. He has undergone a wondrous transformation. He is elegantly dressed, carefully groomed. He speaks as an educated man. NOTE: Although others refer to him as "Monsieur Madeleine" or "Monsieur Mayor," the script will continue to identify him as VALJEAN.)*

FANTINE *(angrily)*. So you're the mayor, are you? The fine and wonderful Monsieur Madeleine. *(She spits in his face.)*

JAVERT. You'll get a year for that!

VALJEAN *(wipes away the spittle)*. Inspector Javert, this woman is to go free.

JAVERT *(astonished)*. To go free?

VALJEAN *(to POLICEMAN)*. Release her. *(POLICEMAN looks to JAVERT, who nods reluctant assent. POLICEMAN releases FANTINE, salutes, exits R. JAVERT waits until he's out before speaking. He can't believe his ears.)*

JAVERT. Monsieur Mayor, the woman cannot go free. She insulted a respected citizen in the street.

VALJEAN. I was crossing the square when you took this woman away. There were still people about and I asked what had happened. I heard the story. *(To FANTINE.)* The flower girl told me about your daughter.

FANTINE *(dazed)*. That's Marguerite for you.

JAVERT. The law is the law. (*Feeling weak, FANTINE suppresses a cough, sits on the stool.*)

VALJEAN. Your "respected citizen" was at fault.

JAVERT. But she has insulted you, too, the mayor of this town!

VALJEAN. That is my affair.

JAVERT. If you'll forgive me, Monsieur Mayor, the insult was not to yourself but to justice. And justice is my affair.

VALJEAN (*to FANTINE*). I am sorry about what happened at the factory. Why didn't you come to me? Never mind. I will pay your debts and arrange for your child to be brought here or else you can go to her. There is no longer a need for you to stay. You may go.

FANTINE (*slowly gets up, weak and bewildered*). You mean it... what you said about my daughter... my Cosette...?

VALJEAN. Yes.

FANTINE. Is such good fortune possible...? (*FANTINE, unable to believe her luck, wearily crosses R and out.*)

JAVERT. I have my duty. Duty requires me to send that woman to prison.

VALJEAN. She will not spend a single day in prison.

JAVERT. There are regulations -- !

VALJEAN. I have the authority over them.

(*POLICEMAN returns.*)

POLICEMAN. Inspector Javert.

JAVERT. What is it?

POLICEMAN. Whe woman has fainted.

VALJEAN. Take her to my factory infirmary. Tell the good sisters I'll be along.

POLICEMAN. Yes, Monsieur Mayor. (*POLICEMAN exits.*)

JAVERT. Justice won't be mocked.

VALJEAN. That's enough. (*Pause, then:*)

JAVERT. I recommend that I be dismissed from my post.

VALJEAN. What in the world are you talking about? Surely, this incident with the poor woman --

JAVERT (*interrupts*). An inferior member of the public service has shown the utmost disrespect for a magistrate. I am duty bound to inform you of the fact.

VALJEAN. Who is the offender?

JAVERT. I am.

VALJEAN. You?

JAVERT. Yes.

VALJEAN. And who is the magistrate?

JAVERT. You are. From the day you came to this town with no past, I had inquiries made. And then there was the incident with Fauchelevent and the cart. Your great strength. A trifle, perhaps, but I suspected you of being a man called Jean Valjean. It is a punishable crime for a convict to assume a false identity.

VALJEAN *(controlled)*. What name?

JAVERT. Jean Valjean. He was a dangerous prisoner when I was a guard at Toulon prison. He had great physical strength. He was to report every week to the local police, but he never did. He broke his parole. He dropped from sight. Well, I believed... anyway, I denounced you to the authorities in Paris.

VALJEAN. What did they say?

JAVERT *(holds up the crumpled letter)*. That I was crazy. They were right.

VALJEAN. I'm glad you realize it.

JAVERT. They must be right, since the real Jean Valjean has been found. *(VALJEAN remains disturbingly calm.)*

VALJEAN. Has he.

JAVERT. They caught him stealing again. They'll go hard on him. Of course, the fellow denies he's Jean Valjean.

VALJEAN. Of course. Where is he now?

JAVERT. In Digne. The trial is tomorrow.

VALJEAN. Javert, you are an honorable man. You are exaggerating your offense against me. I want you to stay in your present post.

JAVERT. I cannot agree to that.

VALJEAN. Well, we shall have to see. *(He holds out his hand.)*

JAVERT. I cannot shake your hand, Monsieur Mayor. That is out of the question. A magistrate does not shake hands with an informer. When I abused my powers as a police officer I became nothing else. I shall continue to perform my duties until I have been replaced. And, now, Monsieur Mayor, if you'll excuse me. *(He exits L.)*

VALJEAN *(to himself)*. I buried you, Jean Valjean. But you have risen from the grave.

SCENE EIGHT

SCENE: *Courtroom. As soon as VALJEAN says the last line of the previous Scene, lights shift and VALJEAN exits. As he does, JUDGE, PROSECUTOR, CHAMPMATHIEU, SERGEANT, POLICEMAN move onstage and take their positions. Some area or railing suggests a witness stand. SPECTATORS also enter, L and R. SERGEANT and POLICEMAN swiftly position the table so it faces out to the audience. Stool or chair behind it. Some SPECTATORS carry in stools, sit. Others sit on bench down R, on the cot. Some stand. PROSECUTOR stands to one side of the table, JUDGE sits behind it. CHAMPMATHIEU, his hands in shackles, stands as the center of attention. Others are positioned for the best Stage Picture. There is a hubbub of AD LIB conversation. The effect of this Scene opening is that the trial is already "in progress," rather than just beginning.*

JUDGE *(banging gavel)*. Be silent! *(Again.)* Silence, I say. *(To PROSECUTOR, when hubbub subsides.)* Continue.

PROSECUTOR *(points to CHAMPMATHIEU)*. The accused is not merely a thief who has been caught stealing apples, but a highly dangerous ruffian, who has been sought by the law since his release from Toulon prison. *(CHAMPMATHIEU is a pitiful sight. In rags, dirty, his hair in disarray. He's dimwitted and incapable of defending himself. As much as possible, he looks like the VALJEAN we got to know in the PRIEST'S cottage.)*

CHAMPMATHIEU. Champmathieu... my name is Champmathieu... my friends call me Monkey... *(Laughter.)*

PROSECUTOR. Your name is Jean Valjean.

CHAMPMATHIEU. Valjean... no, Champmathieu.

PROSECUTOR. I call Madame Rondeau to the witness stand.
JUDGE. Madame Rondeau has already given her deposition.
PROSECUTOR. I wish the court to be absolutely certain.
JUDGE. Very well. *(To SERGEANT.)* Call Madame Rondeau.
SERGEANT *(calls off-stage).* Madame Rondeau!

(On cue, MME. RONDEAU, a matron, enters and moves to the witness railing - or area.)

PROSECUTOR. Madame Rondeau --
MME. RONDEAU. Yes, monsieur?
PROSECUTOR. There is no doubt in your mind that this man is Jean Valjean?
MME. RONDEAU. None.
PROSECUTOR. How can you be so sure?
MME. RONDEAU *(eager to testify).* I remember him well. Some years ago, of course. He came to my inn. He presented his parole papers and I turned him away.

(As the trial proceeds, VALJEAN returns, stands on the sideline, observes.)

MME. RONDEAU. I could never forget that face. I later heard from Mlle. Myriel that he had stolen her brother's candlesticks. *(To CHAMPMATHIEU.)* Thief. *(To JUDGE.)* When they arrested him for stealing the apples I was only too happy to denounce him. He can call himself whatever he wishes, but my eyes never deceive.
JUDGE. Thank you for your testimony, Mme. Rondeau.
MME. RONDEAU. Is that all?
JUDGE. That is all.
MME. RONDEAU. No more questions?
PROSECUTOR. None. *(MME. RONDEAU is disappointed. She likes attention.)*
MME. RONDEAU. As you please. *(She steps aside.)*
PROSECUTOR. I wish to call the prisoner Bibolet.
JUDGE *(to SERGEANT).* The prisoner Bibolet.
SERGEANT. *(calls off-stage).* The prisoner Bibolet!

(BIBOLET enters, dressed in prison garb. He moves to witness area.)

PROSECUTOR. You were in prison with this man? *(Points to CHAMPMATHIEU. BIBOLET nods.)* There is no doubt in your mind that he is the prisoner Jean Valjean? *(BIBOLET nods his head. He has no doubt.)* There, we have it, Your Honor. He has been identified by one of his own.

CHAMPMATHIEU. You're wicked. I'm one of those who don't eat everyday. I stole the apples, yes. But they were lying on the ground. *(Laughter from SPECTATORS.)*

PROSECUTOR *(a step toward CHAMPMATHIEU)*. You're clever, Valjean. But not clever enough. Useless to play the village idiot. You have been trapped. You will be returned to prison and spend the rest of your life there.

VALJEAN. *No! (Murmur of astonishment from SPECTATORS.)*

JUDGE. Who spoke? *(VALJEAN steps forward.)*

VALJEAN. I did. The mayor of Montfermeil.

JUDGE. Monsieur Madeleine? I am honored. You wish to comment on this case?

VALJEAN. That man is not Jean Valjean. *(General consternation.)*

JUDGE *(bangs gavel)*. Silence! Silence, I say. *(Hubbub quiets.)*

PROSECUTOR. Monsieur Mayor, is this some kind of bizarre joke? The prisoner Bibolet has just identified him.

VALJEAN. When a prisoner becomes a witness for the court he is paid twenty-five sous a day. He eats well and he is released from his hard labor for the duration of the trial. A thousand prisoners would swear this dimwitted fellow is Jean Valjean and justice would have nothing to do with it.

JUDGE *(shocked)*. Monsieur Mayor, you astonish me.

PROSECUTOR. Madame Rondeau has also identified the accused.

VALJEAN. I heard. *(Moves to MME. RONDEAU.)* Think back. I carried a sack over one shoulder. Your inn had a bell above the desk. It was broken. I banged on a table and cried out -- "Landlord!" You told me your husband had recently died. You asked where I was from. When I said Toulon you became suspicious. I said, "The law requires me to show you my parole papers." You became alarmed, "Oh, if only my poor husband were still alive!" Then, you told me, get out or you would scream until the police came to evict me. *(The courtroom is hushed, hanging on every word.)* You noticed I had a prison tattoo on my arm. *(He rolls up his sleeve. All strain for a look. CHAMPMATHIEU is mesmerized. VALJEAN holds up his arm for all to see.)* This brands me a prisoner of the state! Criminal! Outcast! Convict! Convict! Convict!

JUDGE. Calm yourself, Monsieur Mayor.

VALJEAN. Send for Monseigneur Myriel. Send for the town priest. He will know me.

JUDGE. Monseigneur Myriel has been dead for some years. *(VALJEAN reacts.)*

VALJEAN. So be it. *(Then:)* I will not send another man to prison in my place. *(Steps close to MME. RONDEAU.)* You do remember.

MME. RONDEAU *(frightened)*. I... I...

VALJEAN. Look at my eyes, my face. I wasn't always a gentleman. You had a bird in a wicker cage. You called it -- "Butterfly." *(MME. RONDEAU gives a short scream.)*

MME. RONDEAU. It's true! It's true! This is Jean Valjean!

AD LIBS. What? Can it be true? It's not possible! Monsieur Mayor!

VALJEAN *(shouts)*. I am Jean Valjean! I am Jean Valjean!

JUDGE *(banging the gavel)*. Silence, silence!

CHAMPMATHIEU *(chuckling)*. What did I tell you? I know who I am. Do I get something to eat?

PROSECUTOR. Enough from you. *(To VALJEAN.)* Monsieur Mayor, a respected citizen like yourself -- do you realize what you are saying? Do you realize what you have done?

VALJEAN. I realize an innocent man will not be convicted. *(To JUDGE.)* I am at your disposal. I will trouble the Court no further. If I am not to be arrested at once I will leave. I have things to attend to. The Court knows who I am and where I live, and can send for me when it chooses. *(He exits. Court is stunned. No one moves.)*

CHAMPMATHIEU. And me? What about me?

JUDGE. You are acquitted.

CHAMPMATHIEU. I don't understand. *(JUDGE bangs the gavel.)*

JUDGE. This trial is ended. *(All exit, L and R. NOTE: As AC-TORS depart the Scene they take all the props with them, so that all that remains onstage is the cot.)*

SCENE NINE

SCENE: *Town street - forestage. Day. MME. VICTURNIEN enters. With her is FAUCHELEVENT. As they converse, MME. GRIBIER, a gossip, comes from other direction. NOTE: FAN-TINE, wearing a white hospital gown, will get onto the cot as this Scene plays. She is aided by SISTER SIMPLICITY. When FANTINE is stretched out, SISTER SIMPLICITY exits, only to return with a pillow and a white sheet or blanket. She places the pillow under FANTINE's head and tucks the sheet or blanket around her, exits.*

MME. VICTURNIEN *(savoring the news)*. A public outrage. I should have known he was too good to be true. Monsieur *Madeleine*, indeed. Ha! Monsieur *Scoundrel*.

FAUCHELEVENT. I don't believe it. Not a word of it.

MME. VICTURNIEN. They're talking about it in every village.

FAUCHELEVENT. How can a saint be an ex-convict? It's not possible!

MME. GRIBIER. Have you heard?

MME. VICTURNIEN. Yes, yes, we've heard. Who hasn't?

MME. GRIBIER. What will become of the factory? The school? The hospital?

FAUCHELEVENT. I still think there's been a mistake. Monsieur Madeleine saved my life. I would have died but for Monsieur Madeleine.

MME. VICTURNIEN. We don't want to hear about that.

MME. GRIBIER. Have they arrested him?

MME. VICTURNIEN. They will. What a disgrace for our town.

MME. GRIBIER. Monsieur Madeleine has brought shame to us all.

MME. VICTURNIEN. When people ask where I'm from, I shall lie.

MME. GRIBIER. So will I.

MME. VICTURNIEN. Why don't we go to the police? Find out what's happening.

MME. GRIBIER. Will they put him in chains?

MME. VICTURNIEN *(starts to exit R).* He's a criminal, isn't he? That's where such creatures belong -- in chains. *(She's out.)*

MME. GRIBIER *(to FAUCHELEVENT).* They say he's murdered people. They say he's been vicious all his life. *(She follows after MME. VICTURNIEN. FAUCHELEVENT is confused by the whole thing.)*

FAUCHELEVENT. How is it possible for a man to sprout horns overnight? *(Shaking his head, sadly exits after the others. Sound: Singing of Christmas Carol from off-stage L, barely audible, dreamlike.)*

SCENE TEN

SCENE: *Hospital room. FANTINE coughs, talks in her troubled sleep.*

FANTINE. Cosette... Cosette...

(Singing fades. SISTER SIMPLICITY enters, checks her patient. FANTINE opens her eyes.)

FANTINE. Oh, it's you, Sister. I was dreaming Cosette was with me.

SISTER SIMPLICITY. You must keep calm, my child. You're very ill.

FANTINE. My dream was so real.

SISTER SIMPLICITY. Sleep.

FANTINE. I thought I heard singing.

SISTER SIMPLICITY. It's Christmas Eve.

FANTINE. I'd forgotten. Imagine such a thing, forgetting Christmas Eve. Next Christmas Cosette and I will be together. We will, won't we? *(She coughs. SISTER SIMPLICITY, to make her breathing easier, helps FANTINE to a sitting position.)*

SISTER SIMPLICITY. Try not to excite yourself. It's bad for your lungs. You know what the doctor said. Do you think you could take some broth?

FANTINE. No, no, I'm not hungry.

(VALJEAN enters from SR. SISTER SIMPLICITY sees him.)

SISTER SIMPLICITY. Monsieur Madeleine?

FANTINE. He's here? *(Sees him.)* You've been away.

VALJEAN. A few moments, Sister.

SISTER SIMPLICITY. She's very weak.

FANTINE. No, I'm not. I'm strong. I get stronger everyday. *(SISTER SIMPLICITY smiles gently, exits. VALJEAN steps to the cot. FANTINE is in a state of nervous excitement.)* When will you go for Cosette? When will you let me see her?

VALJEAN. You must get well first.

FANTINE. Seeing Cosette will make me well. *(Grabs his hand.)* Monsieur, promise me this -- you know what my life has been. Cosette must be spared that. If anything should happen to me --

VALJEAN. You mustn't talk like that.

FANTINE. Promise you'll look after her. Promise you'll protect her.

VALJEAN. As long as I live Cosette will want for nothing.

FANTINE. Ah, what am I thinking of? I'm getting better. I'm sure there's nothing seriously wrong with me. Cosette won't recognize me. She'll have forgotten her mother after all this time. Children have such short memories. Do you think she'll be pretty? *(Coughs badly.)* Oh, Monsieur. *(Clings to him, delirious.)* My Cosette! I can hear her! You have brought her to me. Bless you. We're going to be so happy. I'll have a little garden where she can play... *(Coughs, lies back on the cot, still holding VALJEAN's hand.)* I'll watch while she skips across the grass... *(She stops talking. VALJEAN doesn't realize she's dead. He looks down at her.)*

VALJEAN. Fantine -- ?

(SISTER SIMPLICITY returns.)

SISTER SIMPLICITY *(urgent tone).* the police, Monsieur Mayor. They're here. Save yourself. Go. Quickly.

VALJEAN. Is she -- ? *(SISTER SIMPLICITY checks. Nods sadly that FANTINE is dead. He kisses FANTINE's forehead.)*

SISTER SIMPLICITY. Go, Monsieur. I beg you. *(VALJEAN quickly exits SR. SISTER SIMPLICITY makes the sign of the cross. Pulls the sheet over the dead FANTINE.)*

JAVERT's VOICE *(from off-stage L).* Where are you, Valjean? You won't escape me!

(JAVERT storms into the room.)

SISTER SIMPLICITY. Please, Inspector Javert. Lower your voice. God has taken Mlle. Fantine from us.

JAVERT *(pulls back the sheet).* It'll be a common grave for this one. *(Covers her face.)* Where is he?

SISTER SIMPLICITY. Who, Inspector?

JAVERT. Don't try to protect him. The mayor!

SISTER SIMPLICITY. He is not here.

JAVERT. He was here!

SISTER SIMPLICITY. Yes.

JAVERT. Do you know where he's gone?

SISTER SIMPLICITY. No. *(Without asking permission, SISTER SIMPLICITY exits. JAVERT looks to FANTINE.)*

JAVERT. You'd have been better off if you had gone to prison. *(Stage lighting begins to dim. As this happens, JAVERT steps C, faces audience, speaking as if he meant the world to hear.)* I will find you, Jean Valjean. You will not escape Inspector Javert. I know how your mind works. You lived inside a prison -- *(Bitterly.)* But I was *born* in one. We both stink of the gutter, but I am washing away that stink. You will never be free. Justice will not be mocked. No matter how long it takes -- a year, two. Ten! I will hound you to death. I will sink in my teeth and never let go! *(Music. Lights fade to darkness, leaving JAVERT in the eerie afterglow. END ACT ONE.)*

ACT TWO

Prologue

SETTING: *We get a sweeping view of various "locales" in Paris. DR shows us two rooms in a wretched tenement house. The rooms are divided by a section of broken "wall." The smaller of the two rooms, downstage, displays a writing table with mirror, chair, washstand with basin, pitcher, towel rag, and (if space permits) a small bed or cot. The next room, upstage somewhat, angled for audience sightlines, is much larger. Contains a table, some broken chairs or stools, a torn mattress and/or rags on the floor for sleeping. Perhaps a clothesline with some sad garments hung out. The hallway to the rooms is off-stage R. In contrast, DL exhibits an elegant chair and side table. UL (on a raised platform, if possible), is a desk with a chair behind it. These "views" form something of a semi-circle, broken by an open space UC. A garden bench is positioned SC.*

AT OPENING: *VICTOR H. is discovered seated on the garden bench, back to audience. He rests his chin on his walking stick.*

VICTOR H *(turns).* Ah, there you are. *(Indicates bench.)* When I sit here in the ·Luxembourg Gardens I forget everything. So peaceful. *(Stands.)* It is now ten years later. Paris. The threads of our story interweave like the threads of a tapestry. Jean Valjean has Cosette with him and she has learned not to ask questions.

(VALJEAN and COSETTE, arm and arm, stroll into view from DL on the forestage. VICTOR H. nods to them. They walk UC and out. NOTE: VALJEAN wears a jeweled ring. COSETTE is a lovely teen-age girl.)

VICTOR H. As far as Cosette is concerned, Monsieur Leblanc is her father. "Monsieur Leblanc" is what he now calls him-

40

self. Valjean changes his name as often as he changes his address. *(Moves to desk and chair.)* This is the office of Inspector Javert. He has transferred to the Paris division some months ago. He has never given up his pursuit of Jean Valjean, but at the moment he has no idea his quarry is so close. This is a busy time for Javert. The smell of revolution is in the air. *(Takes a step toward the boarding house, indicates with his walking stick.)* In that wretched tenement house resides the family Thenardier. The inn was lost years ago and they now exist solely by "their wits." In the same way rats in the Paris sewers manage to exist. Or, should I say "survive?" Monsieur Thenardier now calls himself Jondrette. *(Turns to elegant chair and side table.)* Aha, this is an entirely different matter. The house of Mlle. Gillenormand, spinster daughter of that relic of another age -- Monsieur Gillenormand. Rich, arrogant, selfish.

(MARIUS, a rather handsome young man, steps into the "room" reading a pamphlet.)

VICTOR H. That young man is her nephew. Marius. Her only living relative. Two such as these could not be more different. *(As the next scene begins, VICTOR H. strolls casually UC and out.)*

SCENE ONE

SCENE: *House of MLLE. GILLENORMAND.*

MARIUS *(reading pamphlet)*. "France is in great peril. Day by day liberty suffers. Frenchmen, listen to the voice of reason..."

(MLLE. GILLENORMAND, an elderly spinster dogmatic in her beliefs, enters L.)

MLLE. GILLENORMAND. I am surprised you are still at home, Marius. *(Startled by her arrival, MARIUS attempts to hide the pamphlet behind his back.)*

MARIUS. I had forgotten the time.

MLLE. GILLENORMAND. You don't deceive me, nephew.

MARIUS. Deceive?

MLLE. GILLENORMAND. When a young man who has never before displayed an interest in flowers and manicured lawns suddenly becomes a nature-lover -- well, that is, I mean to say --

MARIUS. What are you trying to say, aunt?

MLLE. GILLENORMAND. There must be a young lady in the picture. *(She sits.)*

MARIUS. You're perceptive, aunt. There is a young lady, yes.

MLLE. GILLENORMAND. What is her name?

MARIUS. "Cosette."

MLLE. GILLENORMAND. And when you are together what do you talk about?

MARIUS. I talk of love. Cosette talks of her father. He guards her as if she were made of spun gold. So far, we have had only stolen moments.

MLLE. GILLENORMAND. You've missed your calling, Marius. You should have been a poet.

MARIUS. Cosette makes me feel like a poet.

MLLE. GILLENORMAND. What are you hiding behind your back?

MARIUS. What am I hiding?

MLLE. GILLENORMAND. Please don't parrot my words. A love letter? Hmmmm?

MARIUS. No.

MLLE. GILLENORMAND. Whatever it is, may I see it? *(MARIUS is reluctant. Then --)*

MARIUS. As you wish. *(He hands her the pamphlet. She quickly scans it.)*

MLLE. GILLENORMAND. You're incorrigible. These seditious writings, treasonous! How can you have such slanderous pamphlets in your possession? I have only to look at you to see your father. *(MARIUS tenses.)*

MARIUS. I've asked you before, aunt, please do not criticize my father to me.

MLLE. GILLENORMAND. This is my house and I shall do exactly as I wish. I wish to criticize your father. My late brother was a fool.

MARIUS. My father was a heroic soldier who gallantly served the Republic.

MLLE. GILLENORMAND. Republic! *(To her feet.)* How I detest that word. Burns my tongue to say it. Your father and all those who served the Republic betrayed their lawful king. Traitors, anarchists. They were villains. robbers and murderers.

MARIUS. That's enough. *(Bristles.)* It's obvious, aunt, an aristocrat like yourself and a man who champions freedom cannot live under the same roof.

MLLE. GILLENORMAND. We've been over this before. Too many times.

MARIUS. I've made up my mind.

MLLE. GILLENORMAND. You're being ridiculous, Marius. If you left, how would you support yourself?

MARIUS. That is my concern.

MLLE. GILLENORMAND. Like father, like son.

MARIUS. I take that as high compliment. If he were here now, he would have a pamphlet in his hand. Long live the Republic! *(This is too much for MLLE. GILLENORMAND.)*

MLLE. GILLENORMAND. Clear out! You go too far. *(MARIUS nods curtly, exits. MLLE. GILLENORMAND glares after him, realizes she holds the pamphlet. Angrily, she tears it in two.)* Young fool. *(Exits.)*

SCENE TWO

SCENE: *Luxembourg Gardens. A couple of young CITIZENS enter UC and stroll toward the bench. They are intercepted by ADELE and HENRI, two student revolutionaries, who enter on forestage from DR. They carry pamphlets. They spot the CITIZENS and move for them, pamphlets extended.*

ADELE. Millions in France are hungry!

HENRI. Millions are out of work!

ADELE. Join us in protest.

HENRI. This Sunday. Boulevard de Mars.

ADELE. If we don't get satisfaction -- to the barricades!

HENRI. To the barricades!

ADELE. Take a pamphlet.

HENRI. Read it. Study it. *(The CITIZENS are not only disinterested, they are annoyed. Quickly, they exit in the space between JAVERT's "office" and MLLE. GILLENORMAND's "house.")*

ADELE *(calls after them)*. Don't stick your heads in the sand!

HENRI. Let them go. It's too nice a day for revolution, anyway.

ADELE *(still calling after them)*. Paris is about to explode!

HENRI. To tell the truth, Adele, I'd much rather sit at a cafe table with a glass of red wine.

ADELE. All right, then. Let's.

HENRI. You got any money?

ADELE *(sits on bench)*. Do I ever? You?

HENRI. Flat.

(MARIUS enters DL. He carries some books tied in a bundle.)

HENRI. Hello, look who's here.

ADELE *(all smiles)*. Marius!

HENRI. Just in time to help us distribute these pamphlets.

MARIUS. You and your pamphlets. I sympathize with your cause, Henri, but I'm not ready to work for it.

ADELE. Dilettante.

MARIUS. Perhaps.

ADELE. How are you getting on without your aunt's help?

MARIUS. I'm not helpless, Adele. *(Holds up books.)* I'm translating. From Latin to French. French to German. German to Latin.

HENRI. Ugh.

(As they speak, JAVERT enters UC and pretends he's not studying the group, which of course, he is. A second later and a PLAINCLOTHES POLICEMAN enters. The two converse,

sub rosa. JAVERT indicates that the POLICEMAN should keep a close watch on HENRI and, then, JAVERT turns and exits upstage and off, L.)

ADELE. Found a place to live?

MARIUS. Yes. A foul tenement house down by the river. It's the best I can afford.

HENRI. I know a second-hand dealer who will buy a spare pair of trousers.

ADELE. I know a clockmaker who will buy your watch.

MARIUS. I'm poorly paid, but I can live on what I make.

HENRI. In that case, could you lend me a few sous?

ADELE. We'll all have some wine.

MARIUS. I'm waiting for someone.

ADELE. Your little Cosette who walks with her father? How do you manage to get close?

MARIUS. I leave a note -- *(Indicates.)* -- on this bench. A time and place to meet. Clumsy, I admit, but so far it's worked.

ADELE. Bravo.

MARIUS. Tip a glass for me. *(Takes out some coins, passes them to HENRI.)*

HENRI. Enough for two glasses each, Adele.

ADELE. I never thought your aunt would cut you off.

MARIUS. She's tried to send me money, but I have refused to accept it. When she writes, I don't reply.

HENRI *(good-naturedly)*. Lunatic.

ADELE. Henri is right. You're a lunatic. *(Stands.)* Sure you won't join us?

(COSETTE and VALJEAN have entered the "gardens" from UC. COSETTE has a parasol. Behind them walks a servant, CHARLOTTE.)

MARIUS *(sotto)*. She's here.

ADELE. We're not needed, Henri. *(She yanks him by the arm and the two exit DL. POLICEMAN, discreetly as possible, follows.)*

COSETTE. It's a beautiful day, isn't it, Father?

VALJEAN. Yes, my angel. *(MARIUS quickly sits on the bench and covertly takes a note from some pocket and places it beside him. As VALJEAN and COSETTE approach, MARIUS gets to his feet.)*

MARIUS *(faces them)*. Excuse me, Monsieur, Mademoiselle. Won't you take the bench? *(He gestures to the bench, indicating the spot for COSETTE which, of course, has the note.)*

COSETTE. How kind of you.

VALJEAN. You were here first, young man. Besides, the Gardens have more than enough empty benches.

COSETTE. Oh, but this one is in the sunshine, Father.

MARIUS *(to VALJEAN)*. I've seen you walking here everyday. So, you are no stranger to me. Permit me to introduce myself. My name is Gillenormand. My father was a famous soldier in the Republic. Perhaps you've heard of him?

VALJEAN. No.

MARIUS. My Christian name is Marius.

VALJEAN *(icy)*. Good day, Monsieur. *(Defeated, MARIUS nods to VALJEAN and then to COSETTE. He starts to exit DR.)*

CHARLOTTE. Monsieur Gillenormand. *(MARIUS stops, turns. CHARLOTTE picks up the note.)* Does this belong to you? *(Both MARIUS and COSETTE are disappointed. MARIUS takes the note, again nods to VALJEAN and COSETTE, exits DR.)*

VALJEAN. That young man seems anxious to intrude. If you see him again, Cosette, ignore him. Do you understand?

COSETTE *(reluctant)*. Yes, Father.

VALJEAN *(worried)*. Always be wary of strangers. You haven't spoken with him? You haven't encouraged him in some way?

(COSETTE hesitates. She doesn't want to lie, but she doesn't want to answer. Fortunately, AZELMA, the younger Thenardier daughter, enters on forestage, DL, and interrupts. She's tiny, dressed in a filthy garment, no shoes. Face smudged with soot. She clutches a note in her hand.)

AZELMA. Please, Monsieur. You remember me? Only last week you gave me money for bread. My family lived another day because of your charity.

CHARLOTTE. She's a beggar, Monsieur. They all have these stories. If you give her more money you'll never be rid of her.

COSETTE. Father can't resist when someone's in need. *(AZELMA hands him the note.)*

VALJEAN. This seems to be the day for notes. *(Opens, reads.)* "Excuse me sending my daughter and not coming myself. Alas, the insufficiency of my wardrobe prevents me from going out. If you will be so good as to accompany my daughter you will be witness of a shattered life. I await your visit or your gift. P.S. Even as little as forty sous would help."

CHARLOTTE. Such notes are scattered like confetti.

COSETTE. What a sad letter.

CHARLOTTE. You're not going with the child, Monsieur Leblanc?

VALJEAN. I want to see the truth or lie of this note. Take Cosette home. I won't be long.

AZELMA *(hurries UC)*. Follow me, Monsieur.

VALJEAN. Yes, yes. *(AZELMA runs off, UR. VALJEAN follows.)*

COSETTE. He is such a good man, my father.

CHARLOTTE *(the realist)*. Even a good man can have his throat cut in a dark alley.

COSETTE. Charlotte, you mustn't say such things.

CHARLOTTE. I know Paris, Mademoiselle Cosette. You do not. *(COSETTE and CHARLOTTE exit DL. Strike garden bench.)*

SCENE THREE

SCENE: *MARIUS's room. MARIUS enters from hallway. He has the bundle of books in one hand and a small loaf of bread in the other. He puts the bread and books on the writing table, steps to pitcher, pours water into basin. EPONINE, AZELMA's sister, enters.*

EPONINE. I heard you on the stairs. *(MARIUS turns. EPONINE is as miserably dressed as her sister. Underneath her dirt and look of weariness there's an undercurrent of genuine worth.)* I live next door with my family. I'm your neighbor.

MARIUS. Yes, I know.

EPONINE. We're a noisy family.

MARIUS. I won't argue. *(Washes his hands.)* The wall is thin and cracked.

EPONINE. My name is Eponine. The landlady told me your name. Marius. *(MARIUS dries his hands with the towel, a rag.)*

MARIUS. Is there something you want? *(EPONINE ignores the question. She likes being with MARIUS and wants to stay as long as possible. Sees books on the table.)*

EPONINE. Books! *(Checks the bindings.)* I can read. Write, too. A mirror. You have a mirror! *(She picks it up and studies her reflection.)* I can be pretty when I have something proper to wear and my face is scrubbed. *(Sees.)* Bread. *(Impulsively, hungrily, she starts to twist away a piece. Quickly she stops, knowing MARIUS is watching her.)*

MARIUS. Go ahead. Have some. *(Delighted, EPONINE pulls away the end of the loaf, bites into it with obvious delight.)*

EPONINE. It's fresh! We only get stale and only that when times are good. I'd forgotten the taste. *(MARIUS is doing his best not to be rude, but he wishes she'd go. He sits at the writing table, unstrings the books.)* Last winter, before coming here, we lived beneath bridges. You had to huddle together not to freeze. Sometimes I wanted to drown myself, but then I thought, no, it's too cold. Sometimes I go out at night and stay out until it's dawn. Sometimes I think people are throwing stones at me. When you haven't had anything to eat for days the world seems a very strange place.

MARIUS. I am sorry, Eponine, but I must tend to my work.

EPONINE. We are being turned out. We're behind in our rent.

MARIUS *(resigned)*. How much does it come to?

EPONINE. Twenty francs.

MARIUS *(takes coins from his pocket; to himself)*. First Henri and now you. If this keeps up I'll be driven back to my aunt. *(To EPONINE.)* I have thirty francs. I'll give you twenty-five.

EPONINE. Twenty-five!

MARIUS. Twenty for the rent. Five for some food.

EPONINE. Five francs is enough to stuff us for two days.

MARIUS. I trust you won't make this a habit. My money goes out faster than it comes in. *(Still she doesn't leave.)* What are you waiting for?

EPONINE. I was just thinking, Monsieur, you're not only generous -- you're a good-looking young man. *(She exits. MARIUS thinks about her remark, smiles, gets busy with his work.)*

SCENE FOUR

SCENE: *THENARDIER's room. THENARDIER enters from hallway. We barely recognize him. In rags, dirty, he's lost nothing of his cruel instinct for survival.*

THENARDIER. You haven't made a mistake? If you have I'll whip the skin off your back.

(AZELMA enters behind her father.)

AZELMA. He's coming, I tell you.

THENARDIER. He'd better be.

AZELMA. He'll be here any minute.

THENARDIER. You're sure you got the right mark?

AZELMA. He's the man who always gives money to beggars. He gave me money last week. I told you about him. On Sundays he gives away coins outside the church.

THENARDIER *(thinking, thinking)*. I remember. He must be a Rothschild the way he spends. *(Grabs AZELMA by the ear.)* Pay attention.

AZELMA. Ow! Ow, Father! You're hurting me!

THENARDIER. When this rich fool gets here, cough a little, look sad. Misery makes money. Understand?

AZELMA. I'll look miserable, I promise, but let me go.

THENARDIER. Remember my words, Azelma. *(He releases her and she scurries to the pile of rags and sits like a beaten pup.)*

VALJEAN's VOICE *(from hallway).* May I enter?

THENARDIER *(reacts).* Indeed, sir, you may. An honor.

(VALJEAN enters, looks about, satisfying his curiosity. THENARDIER pulls forth a stool.)

THENARDIER. Do sit down, Monsieur. The stool wobbles, but it's the best I can offer. *(VALJEAN sits. THENARDIER gives a hard look to AZELMA. She coughs.)* My younger daughter has told me of your kindness. Poor thing. She has bad lungs. Without good food and some doctor's care, she will surely be gone come summer.

VALJEAN. A large family?

THENARDIER. Too large, I'm afraid. Too many mouths to feed. Times have not been good to me. Often I say to myself, "Ah, Jondrette, you might as well end it. Better a quick death than a slow one." *(NOTE: VALJEAN doesn't recognize THENARDIER, but THENARDIER has studied VALJEAN from the instant of his entrance. He is trying to place him.)* Another daughter has cut her foot badly. It's black and swollen. My little boy has run away. And my wife is ill. Poor woman got up and went into the street to see if she might beg something to eat. *(AZELMA coughs. THENARDIER indicates his miserable quarters.)* You see how it is. If we do not have the rent by tonight, it's the streets for Jondrette and family.

VALJEAN. Four francs is all I have on me at the moment. I left home without my wallet.

THENARDIER. The rent must be paid by eight.

VALJEAN. Then I'll come at six and I'll bring you sixty francs.

THENARDIER. My noble benefactor!

VALJEAN. Until this evening, then.

THENARDIER. Six o'clock.

VALJEAN. Precisely.

THENARDIER. You are a fine gentleman, sir. Oh, if only you had known me in better days. Why, we might have been friends.

(As VALJEAN starts to leave, MME. THENARDIER hurries in from hallway, also in rags.)

MME. THENARDIER *(a curtsy)*. Monsieur.

THENARDIER. Forgive me. I don't know your name.

VALJEAN. Monsieur Leblanc.

THENARDIER. Monsieur Leblanc has been sent from heaven. We are saved.

MME. THENARDIER. Saved? Oh, Monsieur! We are so grateful. *(VALJEAN nods, exits. When he's gone --)*

AZELMA *(gets up)*. What did I tell you. He's rich!

THENARDIER *(sits at table)*. I hope so. Sixty francs is nothing.

MME. THENARDIER. Nothing?! Have you lost your senses? Sixty francs! He's going to give us sixty francs. A fortune!

THENARDIER. You stupid woman. Didn't you recognize him?

MME. THENARDIER. Should I?

THENARDIER. Think back. Ten years back. The inn. The man who came for Cosette. The man who paid fifteen hundred francs to take her away.

MME. THENARDIER. The man they said was the mayor of Montfermeil?

THENARDIER. He *was* the mayor. If I had known when he came for Cosette the price would have been ten thousand. Twenty!

MME. THENARDIER. But he disappeared. They say he died.

THENARDIER. I don't care what others say. He is the mayor. He is the escaped convict.

MME. THENARDIER. We'll be rich! *(She and AZELMA join hands and dance about.)*

AZELMA. Rich! Rich! We'll be rich! *(Drawn by the noise in the next room, MARIUS gets up and steps to the wall where, supposedly, there's a crack. He pantomimes "peeking" through the crack, listens.)*

THENARDIER. Stop dancing about! I need to think.

MME. THENARDIER *(a horrible thought)*. What if he won't pay up?

THENARDIER. He'll pay for silence. I'll keep him on the hook forever. When he gets here tonight, I'll take his wallet and his pocket watch and anything else I fancy. Did you see that ring on his finger? Worth plenty.

AZELMA. He might put up a struggle.

THENARDIER. If he puts up a struggle, we'll break his neck and drop him in the river. Tonight at six o'clock. *(Alarmed, MARIUS quickly exits from his room, into hallway.)*

AZELMA *(musing)*. That pretty girl in the park, the one he's always with?

MME. THENARDIER. What about her?

AZELMA. She wears lovely clothes. Sometimes flowers in her hair. Do you think she might be Cosette?

MME. THENARDIER. Cosette? That brat! Wearing pretty clothes while my daughters wear rags.

THENARDIER. Find Eponine. We've got work. *(AZELMA and MME. THENARDIER exit room. THENARDIER goes to the rags and from beneath them he pulls out a blackjack or piece of lead pipe. He "tests" it by slapping it against the palm of his hand. Thinking aloud.)* No matter what, I get the wallet, the ring and the watch.

SCENE FIVE

SCENE: *JAVERT's office. As THENARDIER says his last line in Scene Four, JAVERT enters his office from SL. Sits at desk. MARIUS enters from UC, crosses to desk.*

MARIUS. They said the Superintendent wasn't here, but if it was urgent I could speak with the Inspector in charge.

JAVERT *(no attempt at civility)*. I am the Inspector in charge -- Javert. What do you want?

MARIUS. I rent quarters in the building belonging to Madame Minette.

JAVERT. I know the building.

MARIUS. My neighbor is a hard man, unpleasant to his family. He forces his wife and daughters to beg. They give notes to people in the street.

JAVERT. Your neighbor's name is Jondrette. A petty criminal.

MARIUS. You're well informed, Inspector.

JAVERT. I know my job. Continue.

MARIUS. He plans to rob some man who is coming to his rooms.

JAVERT. Do you know the victim?

MARIUS. No. I overheard Jondrette discussing the plan with his wife. If the man puts up a struggle, they plan to kill him.

JAVERT. Was any time mentioned?

MARIUS. Six o'clock.

JAVERT. I will attend to the matter. *(Checks pocket watch.)* Half past four.

MARIUS. If you'll take my advice, Inspector, you won't go alone.

JAVERT. I repeat, monsieur, I know my job. One thing before you leave --

MARIUS. Yes?

JAVERT. -- your name?

MARIUS. Marius Gillenormand.

JAVERT. Gillenormand? An honorable name. A word of advice. It's unwise these days to have radical friends. The Luxembourg Gardens is no place for talk of barricades.

MARIUS *(amazed)*. Your eyes are everywhere, Inspector.

JAVERT. And my ears. *(Checks his pocket watch again.)* Six o'clock?

MARIUS *(confirms)*. Six o'clock. *(JAVERT exits, SL. MARIUS is astonished that one man could know so much. As MARIUS exits UCR, THENARDIER returns to his room and sits at the table.)*

SCENE SIX

SCENE: *THENARDIER's room. MME. THENARDIER hurries in.*

MME. THENARDIER. Azelma saw him coming down the alley.

THENARDIER. Where's Eponine?

MME. THENARDIER. She wants no part of it.

THENARDIER. What's the matter with that girl?

MME. THENARDIER. Don't you know? It's the young gentleman next door. The one who has a little money. She's lovesick.

THENARDIER. Lovesick? Ha! I'll soon knock that out of her. Where are the others?

MME. THENARDIER. In the hallway. Ready when you give the signal.

THENARDIER. Sit down.

MME. THENARDIER. Done.

(She sits. Both keep their eyes on the "door." As they wait, JAVERT appears at SL. With him are PLAINCLOTHES POLICEMEN #1 and #2. Each carries a pistol. They move SC. JAVERT directs POLICEMAN #1 to exit DR. He does. Directs POLICEMAN #2 to exit UC. He does, moving OR. Casually, JAVERT also moves UC. He looks about to ascertain that he's not being watched, moves after POLICEMAN #2.)

MME. THENARDIER. What's keeping him?

THENARDIER. Quiet. *(A rapping at the "door.")*

VALJEAN's VOICE. It's Monsieur Leblanc.

MME. THENARDIER *(stands)*. Come in, Monsieur Leblanc. The door has no lock.

(VALJEAN enters.)

MME. THENARDIER. How punctual you are.

VALJEAN. Those men in the hallway -- ?

MME. THENARDIER. Neighbors, monsieur. Pay them no attention.

VALJEAN. You have dangerous-looking neighbors.

THENARDIER. When you are poor you can't choose who you live next to. *(MME. THENARDIER goes to the pile of rags and from beneath it pulls out an old wooden sign.)* My wife has a valuable painting.

VALJEAN. I have no interest in paintings.

MME. THENARDIER. It is a masterpiece, my dear sir. A picture of great price. *(She hands it to VALJEAN.)* We have been reduced to such straits that we are forced to part with it.

VALJEAN. It's not a picture. It's an old sign. Looks like it belonged to some inn or tavern.

MME. THENARDIER. Yes, yes. *(Hint of menace.)* Perhaps you've seen it before?

VALJEAN. It's worth about three francs. I have no use for it. *(THENARDIER stands and moves to the "door," thus blocking any fast exit by VALJEAN.)*

THENARDIER. You have your wallet with you?

VALJEAN *(sits at table, puts down sign)*. I have.

THENARDIER. For that sign I will accept no less than -- a thousand crowns.

MME. THENARDIER. If you do not buy our "picture," noble benefactor, then we shall denounce you to the police. *(VALJEAN sits perfectly still. THENARDIER moves to the table, puts his knuckles to the wood and stares directly into the face of VALJEAN.)*

THENARDIER. Don't you recognize me?

VALJEAN. No.

THENARDIER. My name isn't Jondrette.

MME. THENARDIER. Anymore than your name is Leblanc. My husband and I ran the inn not far from Montfermeil. Now do you recognize us?

VALJEAN. No more than before.

THENARDIER. You're a cool one, but it won't work. It was Christmas Eve.

MME. THENARDIER. You were disguised, wearing an old overcoat. We thought you were a tramp.

THENARDIER. I recognized you the minute you shoved your face in this room.

MME. THENARDIER. As though butter wouldn't melt in his mouth.

THENARDIER. For fifteen hundred francs you got hold of a girl who was mine and who certainly had rich connections.

MME. THENARDIER. We could have lived off Cosette for the rest of our lives. The spoiled brat. We were too good to her.

THENARDIER. Pay up, Monsieur *Madeleine.*

VALJEAN. I could go to the police.

THENARDIER. Ha!

MME. THENARDIER. You can't play that game. It's you the police are after, not us.

THENARDIER. The money, or I call in my "dangerous" neighbors and they will work you over for a franc apiece.

MME. THENARDIER. They're good at breaking noses. You won't know yourself in the mirror.

VALJEAN *(calmly)*. If you cry out, Madame Thenardier, I will snap your husband's spine.

MME. THENARDIER. How's that? *(Before THENARDIER knows what is happening, VALJEAN has seized his throat in a vise-like grip. As he makes the grab across the table top, VAL-JEAN rises from the stool. THENARDIER gasps, struggling for breath.)*

VALJEAN. One cry, Madame, and you are a widow.

MME. THENARDIER *(gasps)*. Oh, oh! *(With that incredible strength, VALJEAN forces THENARDIER to his knees. The miserable man continues to struggle for breath.)*

VALJEAN. Listen to me well, both of you. If you should bring any unhappiness to my angel, to my Cosette, I will seek you out, together, or one by one *--and slit your throats.*

MME. THENARDIER. Oh!

VALJEAN. For myself I care nothing. For Cosette I care more than you could hope to understand.

MME. THENARDIER *(sobs)*. Let him go, Monsieur. I beg you. Please.

VALJEAN. I didn't survive prison not to know how to deal with scum like you. The choice is yours.

(Sounds of police whistles from off-stage. AZELMA runs in.)

AZELMA. The police are here! We're in for it! *(VALJEAN releases his grip and runs out the door. THENARDIER collapses. MME. THENARDIER dashes to him and checks to see if he's still alive. He is -- because his gasps are audible. Rough voices from off-stage. The POLICEMEN vs. the unseen "dangerous neighbors.")*

MME. THENARDIER. What'll we say? What'll we do?

AZELMA. I don't want to go to jail!

MME. THENARDIER. Shut up. This is all your fault, you wretched girl. You brought that "benefactor" here.

AZELMA. You told me to!

MME. THENARDIER *(helps THENARDIER to his feet)*. You'll be all right.

(JAVERT appears in "doorway.")

JAVERT. Up to your old tricks again, eh, Jondrette?

MME. THENARDIER. We've done nothing wrong.

JAVERT. We've got your pals. Now we've got you. Your victim, the man who ran out. Who was he?

MME. THENARDIER. How should we know? Some fool with too much money for his own good.

JAVERT. Why did he run off? Why didn't he cry out?

THENARDIER. Maybe he didn't want to meet the police.

JAVERT. Devil take it! He must have been the best of the lot. *(He waves the family into the hallway. They shuffle out, dejected. JAVERT trails. NOTE: Reset garden bench.)*

SCENE SEVEN

SCENE: *Luxembourg Gardens. Night. MARIUS enters DR. A moment passes and COSETTE appears, DL.*

COSETTE. Marius. *(He sees her, stands. They embrace, kiss.)*

MARIUS. I was afraid you wouldn't be here.

COSETTE. It's not easy to leave the house without my father seeing me. I don't like to deceive him.

MARIUS. You haven't told him about us?

COSETTE. No. He doesn't think I have anyone, not even a friend. We've always lived like that. Moving from place to place, never staying long. *(Clings to him.)* Oh, Marius.

MARIUS. What is it? What's wrong? *(He guides her to the bench. They sit.)*

COSETTE. We're going away.

MARIUS. What do you mean?

COSETTE. He says we must leave France. He is getting passage for England.

MARIUS. But why? *Why* must you leave France?

COSETTE. He seems terribly worried about something. What does it matter? We're leaving and that is that. *(She fights to hold back tears.)*

MARIUS. No, I won't have it. *(Resolute.)* I know what must be done.

COSETTE. What can be done?

MARIUS. I will get my aunt's permission to marry you.

COSETTE *(overjoyed)*. You mean it? Is such a thing possible? *(Stands beside him.)*

MARIUS. But of course. Your father will have to let you stay. A man and wife cannot be separated. I will see my aunt at once. You will meet me here tomorrow. Noon. Can you manage it?

COSETTE. I'll be here, Marius.

MARIUS. I'll see you to your house. *(MARIUS takes her arm. As they start to exit DL.)*

COSETTE. Father won't object. I know he won't.

MARIUS. They'll both agree. You'll see. My aunt and your father both.

(As they start to exit, VALJEAN steps into view from DR. He does not wish to be seen, but it's plain he's watching from a distance. He waits until the young lovers move off and, then, turns and exits.)

SCENE EIGHT

SCENE: *House of MLLE. GILLENORMAND. MLLE. GIL-
LENORMAND enters from SL talking over her shoulder to
some unseen servant.*

MLLE. GILLENORMAND. You may tell my nephew, yes. I
will receive him. *(Grandly, she settles into the elegant chair
and strikes a pose, muttering to herself.)* Ungrateful boy. Come
to apologize, no doubt. Well, I will not be uncharitable, no.
Youth is youth and Marius is no exception.

(MARIUS enters, steps in front of his aunt, bows.)

MARIUS. Aunt.
MLLE. GILLENORMAND. Very well, I accept your apology.
MARIUS. Apology, aunt? What apology?
MLLE. GILLENORMAND. I know where you've been living
and how you support yourself. By now, you realize how
foolish your independence is. Not only foolish, but something
far worse -- unnecessary. *(She extends her hand.)* You may
kiss me now. *(Changes her mind, taps her cheek.)* No, here. A
fair exchange. One kiss for a healthy measure of forgiveness.
MARIUS. I have not come, aunt, to be forgiven.
MLLE. GILLENORMAND *(snaps)*. Then why have you come?
You never answer my letters and you spurn my money.
MARIUS. I assure you, aunt, from now on I will write everyday.
Or, at least, every week. As for money, I have a great need of
it.
MLLE. GILLENORMAND *(wary)*. You're not gambling?
That's a sure road to ruin.
MARIUS. I don't gamble -- unless you consider marriage a
gamble.
MLLE. GILLENORMAND *(cold)*. Marriage?
MARIUS. I told you about the girl.
MLLE. GILLENORMAND *(critical)*. What do you really know
of the creature?

MARIUS. I know that I love her and she loves me. We have no wish to be parted. But I have seen poverty and what it does to people. We must have money.

MLLE. GILLENORMAND. Go to her family.

MARIUS. She has only her father and I could not ask him.

MLLE. GILLENORMAND. So you come to me. I will not pretend to be annoyed. In fact, this Cosette might be good for you. You've always been too serious. I am a woman of the world and understand such matters. You are still young and still naive. In later years, a "suitable" marriage with a suitable young woman can be arranged. A young woman with her own wealth and from a good line.

MARIUS. A good line? I wish to marry Cosette, not a race horse.

MLLE. GILLENORMAND. Be sensible.

MARIUS. I repeat, I wish to marry Cosette.

MLLE. GILLENORMAND. Never! If you cannot live without this girl, make her your mistress, but your wife -- *never!* *(MARIUS cannot control his anger.)*

MARIUS. A few weeks ago you insulted my father. Tonight you have insulted my future wife. I am sorry to have troubled you. I shall ask nothing more of you. *(MARIUS nods, exits. MLLE. GILLENORMAND gets to her feet. She doesn't wish the meeting to end on this note, pleads after him.)*

MLLE. GILLENORMAND. Marius, don't leave like this! What have I done? He's going away again. This time he'll never come back! Marius... *(She's out. Sound: As MLLE. GIL-LENORMAND exits and the stage lighting shifts, we hear a drum roll in the distance. Sound of drum roll carries over into beginning of next scene.)*

SCENE NINE

SCENE: *Luxembourg Gardens. Following day. Great excitement. CITIZENS enter from DR and DL. HENRI, carrying a rifle in his grip, leads them. They move UC. The drum roll grows louder and louder. Some CITIZEN carries a rolled-up French flag or banner.*

HENRI *(as he moves)*. If we stay together, we'll win the day.

(He waves CITIZENS to follow him. He exits UCR. CITIZENS, too. As the small mob makes its upstage cross, a dejected MARIUS, looking disheveled, enters on forestage from DL. He sits on the bench, ignoring the turmoil. EPONINE, a rifle in her grip, enters DR, sees MARIUS. Sound of drums fades.)

EPONINE. Monsieur Marius.

MARIUS *(looks up)*. Oh, it's you.

EPONINE. Have you come to join in the fight?

MARIUS. Barricades are going up?

EPONINE. Yes.

MARIUS. Aren't you afraid of being killed?

EPONINE. No. *(She moves to him; notices.)* You have a button off your jacket. I'll mend it for you.

MARIUS. If you're not afraid of death, why should I be?

(ADELE enters DR.)

ADELE. I knew we could count on you Marius. We need everyone we can find. Don't sit there. There's work to be done. Sound: Distant gunfire.) They're getting closer. *(She exits UC.)*

EPONINE. No, Monsieur. Battles like this aren't for a gentleman like you. You look so sad. I wish there was something I could do for you.

MARIUS *(sudden thought)*. There is. Promise you won't fail me.

EPONINE. Whatever it is, I promise. *(MARIUS stands, puts his hands to her shoulders.)*

MARIUS. Any minute a young woman will come looking for me. Everyday she comes to the Gardens with her father.

EPONINE. You were with her last night. Here.

MARIUS *(amazed)*. You saw us together?

(VALJEAN enters DR. As in previous scene, he holds back, observes.)

EPONINE. Sometimes I watch you when you don't know I'm there.

MARIUS. But why? Never mind. There's no time. Tell her my aunt refuses her permission. We cannot marry. Tell her if I can't have her for my wife, life is meaningless to me.

(ADELE enters again. This time she, too, has a rifle.)

ADELE. Marius, what are you waiting for? We need you! *She exits. MARIUS looks DL.)*

MARIUS. I can see her. You won't forget?

EPONINE. I am not a child. But if she's to be here in a moment, why not wait and tell her yourself?

MARIUS. We will never see each other again. Not in this life, anyway. *(MARIUS starts to go after ADELE, UC, thinks of something.)* Oh. *(Steps back to EPONINE, takes a coin from his pocket, hands it to her.)* For your trouble. *(He exits. EPONINE stares after him.)*

EPONINE *(softly to herself)*. I don't want your money.

(She drops the coin. COSETTE enters DL, gets a fleeting glimpse of MARIUS in the near distance.)

COSETTE. Marius!

EPONINE. I have a message for you, Mademoiselle. From Monsieur Marius. *(COSETTE doesn't like the sound of EPONINE's words.)*

COSETTE. You are a friend of his?

EPONINE. A neighbor.

COSETTE *(afraid of what she might hear)*. And what... what is the message?

EPONINE. His aunt refuses her permission... he cannot marry... he says... if he can't have you for his wife... life is meaningless.

COSETTE *(knowing the answer)*. Where has he gone?

EPONINE. To meet his death. Like the rest of us. On the barricade.

(COSETTE stifles a gasp. EPONINE, unaffected by COSETTE's reaction, moves UC and out. VALJEAN quickly steps to COSETTE. She is too much in shock to be startled by his appearance.)

VALJEAN. I'll take you home. You never should have come here. I warned you about that young man.

COSETTE. I love him, Father!

VALJEAN. No, you do not.

COSETTE. You can help him. Save him.

VALJEAN. After living all these years, suffering everything that can be suffered, growing old without having ever been young, living without wife or children or friends, after returning good for evil, kindness for cruelty -- am I to lose my angel and with her my whole life, all the happiness I have ever had, simply because some young idiot has captured her heart?

COSETTE *(simply)*. I love him.

VALJEAN *(pause)*. This is the moment I have always dreaded. *(Suddenly, his manner changes, all business.)* Go home. Stay there. If I can, I will save your Marius. *(Happy, COSETTE turns and runs off, DL. Stage lighting shifts to a reddish hue. Sound: Drum roll, building louder and louder until it is deafening.)*

SCENE TEN

SCENE: *The barricade. NOTE: This is simply an extension of the previous scene. The audience should not get a "clear view" of the action... the reddish "hue" represents bursts of artillery. An obstruction or fortification is quickly thrown up by CITIZENS who enter UC, L and R. Flags and banners are unfurled. NOTE: Consult Production Notes on building the barricade. The barricade is positioned SC. Mostly, CITIZENS stand behind the barricade with rifles pointing in the direction of an "unseen" enemy. While the barricade business is going on, sound of deafening drum roll, and/or gunfire, continues. Principals involved at the barricade include: HENRI, ADELE, MARIUS,*

EPONINE and JAVERT, who is in his shirt-sleeves pretending to be one of the mob. VALJEAN takes off his coat and tosses it off-stage.

VALJEAN *(to HENRI)*. Give me a rifle.

HENRI. Gladly. *(Hands rifle to VALJEAN.)*

EPONINE *(to ADELE)*. That man is not one of us. He's a police spy.

ADELE. Who?

EPONINE *(points to JAVERT)*. That one.

ADELE. Henri, did you hear?

JAVERT. The girl's lying. I am not a policeman.

MARIUS. His name is Javert. Inspector Javert. What Eponine says is true.

ADELE. Search him. He must have some identification.

JAVERT. There is no need. I am Inspector Javert.

MARIUS. We'd better lock him up, Henri.

ADELE. Are you mad?! He's a police spy. He can point his finger at each one of us if the battle goes against us.

HENRI. Adele's right. He must be executed.

VALJEAN *(steps forward)*. I am an old soldier of the Republic. Let me have the honor of executing this spy.

HENRI. This is war. You have permission to execute the spy.

VALJEAN *(takes JAVERT by the arm)*. Come with me. *(NOTE: At this point, all except JAVERT and VALJEAN have positioned themselves behind the barricade. The lighting is such that the barricade is in silhouette. A soft light or spot is focused extreme DR and it is to this area that VALJEAN conveys his prisoner. ALL at the barricade freeze so nothing will distract from the VALJEAN-JAVERT dialogue. Sound effects fade under.)*

JAVERT. After all these years, after all my searching, it ends here. The hunter becomes the hunted. I underestimated you. Take your revenge, Valjean. A knife would suit you better than a rifle. *(Pause.)*

VALJEAN. You're free to go. *(JAVERT stares at VALJEAN open-mouthed.)* I don't suppose I shall leave here alive, but if I do, you can find me at Number Seven, rue de l'Homme. I call myself Monsieur Leblanc. Now go.

JAVERT. Why are you doing this?

VALJEAN. That is my concern.

JAVERT. I have failed in my duty. I'd rather you killed me.

VALJEAN. Clear out. *(VALJEAN returns to the barricade. JAVERT watches him for a moment, exits DR. To HENRI.)* It's done. I've killed him.

(Sound: Sudden burst of gunfire or exploding shells. Flashes of red light to simulate artillery. In the shadowy "battle" we see two clear casualties -- EPONINE is shot down and MARIUS is struck by a fusillade. Lights and sound effects go wild. From behind the barricade, VALJEAN drags or half-carries the badly wounded MARIUS. They exit L. For several moments more the "battle" continues. Then, the effects begin to fade and, wearily, CITIZENS take away the barricade, banners, garden bench and as they do, in the DR light returns JAVERT. He gives his monologue directly to the audience.)

JAVERT. "You're free to go... You can find me at Number Seven rue de l'Homme..." Who is Valjean to give me my life? Who allowed him such authority over me? What purpose can life hold when a man such as I is confused? What is justice? What is injustice? You have confused me, Valjean. You have taken a life that had no room for doubt and you have made doubt part of it. You give me my life? You give Javert *nothing!* I thank you for nothing, Jean Valjean. *(Softly.) Damn you!*

(He strides off, DR and VICTOR H. casually strolls into view from UC, looking in the direction of the departed JAVERT. Gradually the "warlike" lighting is replaced by something more comforting.)

VICTOR H. Alas, poor Javert. He was not transformed by Valjean's act of mercy. He was exasperated by it. He was not used to confronting the unknown. The unexpected in human nature was beyond him. He was wholly at a loss. In what was he to believe? He walked to the railing high above the river. He leaned forward and dropped into the darkness. There was a splash, and that was all. *(Happy laughter from OL. VICTOR*

H. indicates with his walking stick.) At Mlle. Gillenormand's the picture is much happier. Marius survived. Valjean escaped the police by traveling through the sewers and depositing his burden on the aunt's doorstep. In only a few weeks he was fully recovered. *(Waltz music.)* Life goes on. *(He strolls DR, off.)*

SCENE ELEVEN

SCENE: *House of Mlle. Gillenormand. Music up and waltzing couples (WEDDING GUESTS) appear from SL and dance about (at least two pair). The lighting is cheerful. As the GUESTS waltz, the music fades, and eventually, the GUESTS wander from view. MARIUS enters L. He is handsomely dressed. Behind him is CHARLOTTE.*

MARIUS. You did the right thing, Charlotte.

CHARLOTTE. If he hadn't taken a turn for the worse I wouldn't have come. On this day of all days. I don't know what to say to little Cosette.

MARIUS. You will say nothing.

CHARLOTTE. I think the doctors are wrong. He's dying of a broken heart. That's his sickness.

MARIUS. Thank you for coming.

CHARLOTTE. You will tell her?

MARIUS. I must return to my guests.

CHARLOTTE. There isn't much time. *(CHARLOTTE senses MARIUS wants her to leave. She curtsies.)* Monsieur. *(She exits DR.)*

MLLE. GILLENORMAND's VOICE *(from OL)*. Marius.

(MLLE. GILLENORMAND enters wearing a fancy gown.)

MLLE. GILLENORMAND. Marius, there's a woman here who says she must speak with you.

MARIUS. It's Charlotte and I've already spoken with her.

MLLE. GILLENORMAND. No, not Charlotte. I don't like the looks of this one, but she's very insistent. You'd better speak with her, otherwise she'll never leave. What will the guests say? *(Before MARIUS can protest, MLLE. GILLENORMAND calls OL.)*

MLLE. GILLENORMAND. This way, madame.

(MME. THENARDIER enters.)

MME. THENARDIER. What a day, what a day. *(MLLE GILLENORMAND exits. MME. THENARDIER is dressed simply, but neatly -- with a rather pretty shawl over her shoulders.)*

MARIUS. I hardly expected to see you again, Madame Jondrette. By the looks of you, you've come up in the world. *(Harsh.)* I understand you and your husband made profits by robbing the bodies at the barricades.

MME. THENARDIER. A vicious rumor. You shouldn't say such things. After all, my little boy and my Eponine both died at the barricades.

MARIUS *(curt)*. What is it you want?

MME. THENARDIER. I have some information to sell.

MARIUS. Whatever it is I'm not interested.

MME. THENARDIER. You will be. It's about your father-in-law. A few gold coins will seal my lips forever. You see, my husband and I are leaving France. We're going to enter the slave trade. There's a lot of money to be made in the slave trade.

MARIUS. Barricades go up and barricades come down. But you and your husband manage to sink to top. *(Brisk.)* My father-in-law is close to dying. He never comes to this house because I have asked him not to.

MME. THENARDIER. Aha, then you know he is an ex-convict?

MARIUS. I know only that he murdered Inspector Javert. Calling it "execution" changes nothing. That is why he is not welcome here. I thank him for saving my life, I thank him for all he has done for my wife, but I can never be friends with a murderer.

MME. THENARDIER. So smug. You are a fool.

MARIUS. Get out.

MME. THENARDIER. Your wife's "father" didn't murder anyone. Javert drowned himself. Everyone knows that.

MARIUS *(stunned)*. I hadn't heard... I was ill for so long. Can it be true?

MME. THENARDIER. Don't take my word for it. Go to the police. They'll tell you.

(COSETTE enters L. She wears a wedding gown. She doesn't recognize MME. THENARDIER, but the woman gives the bride an appraising look, nonetheless.)

COSETTE. Everyone's waiting. Time to cut the cake.

MARIUS. Tell the footman to give you one gold coin. That is the last you will ever get from this house.

MME. THENARDIER *(pleased)*. You are generous. And, Madame Gillenormand --

COSETTE. Yes?

MME. THENARDIER. -- you don't remember me, do you?

COSETTE. Should I?

MME. THENARDIER. Perhaps it's better this way. *(She nods, exits.)*

COSETTE. Who was she?

MARIUS. Never mind about her. Listen to me, Cosette. I've done your father a grave injustice. He never comes here because I won't allow it.

COSETTE. What are you saying? He doesn't come here because he's very ill. I would have postponed the wedding, but he wouldn't hear of it.

MARIUS. Charlotte was here a moment ago. I wasn't going to tell you.

COSETTE. He's worse?

MARIUS. He's dying, Cosette. *(COSETTE reacts. Pause, then.)*

COSETTE. Then we must go to him. *(She starts to exit. MARIUS, ashamed of himself, doesn't move. COSETTE stops, turns, holds out her hand.)* We must go to him -- together. *(MARIUS takes her hand. They exit.)*

SCENE TWELVE

SCENE: *Open stage. The lighting dims. Music. CHARLOTTE enters upstage with a small chair. She places it C, exits DR. As this business plays, ACTORS slowly enter from L and R and position themselves much as they were in the opening moments of the Act One Prologue. Again, they are like shadows. As the shadows move into place, VALJEAN appears DR wearing a long robe. He walks with the aid of a cane and CHAR-LOTTE's assistance. She guides him to the chair. He sits, CHARLOTTE stands behind him. He is breathing heavily. MONSEIGNEUR MYRIEL, a ghost from the past, steps from the dimness, prayer book in hands. Silently, he reads. COSETTE and MARIUS enter from DL. COSETTE goes to VALJEAN, kneels beside him. Music out.*

COSETTE. Father.

VALJEAN. My angel. *(Weak.)* You, Marius, come close, too.

MARIUS *(ashamed)*. I have done you a disservice.

VALJEAN. Whatever you think you've done, it's over. How sweet it is to die like this. You must enjoy life, children. *(MARIUS steps closer.)* Cosette, I have left you two candle-sticks on the mantelpiece. They are made of silver, but to me they are made of gold... you must bury me in any plot of ground that comes handy and put a stone to mark the spot... no name on the stone... I want no name... that is my wish... *(Weaker.)* If my angel -- Cosette -- *(His hand on her head.)* -- cares to visit it sometimes, I shall be glad... *(He dies.)*

MARIUS. Father -- ?

(COSETTE kisses VALJEAN quietly, sobs. VICTOR H. steps from shadows, his voice crisp and businesslike.)

VICTOR H. He got his wish. The stone was quite unadorned. But many years ago someone chalked four lines of verse on it. By now the wind and weather have done their worst and the lines have vanished entirely.

ALL *(softly, choral speech)*.
"He sleeps. although so much he was denied,
He lived; and when his dear love left him, died.

It happened of itself, in the calm way
That in the evening night -- time follows day."
VICTOR H *(to VALJEAN)*. You've earned your rest. Sleep well, Jean Valjean. *(He puts his walking stick over one shoulder and exits scene. Tableau. Music. Lights fade.)*

END OF PLAY

PRODUCTION NOTES

PROPERTIES - ACT ONE

On Stage: Bench (THENARDIER inn). Multi-purpose table with pair of silver candlesticks and two (2) stools (cottage). Another bench -- wide enough to represent a small bed or cot (cottage, hospital).

Brought on:

Prologue: Sack (VALJEAN)

Scene 1: Coins (MME. MAGLIORE)

Scene 2: Cleric's cap, prayer book, match (MONSEIGNEUR MYRIEL); bowl, spoon, bread, glass of wine (MLLE. BAPTIS-TINE); sack, yellow papers (VALJEAN)

Scene 3: Bowl with potatoes, knife (MME. THENARDIER); papers (THENARDIER); infant in blanket (doll), traveling bag (FANTINE)

Scene 4: Hand bell (MME. VICTURNIEN); straw basket with cups, bread, bottle of wine (FAUCHELEVENT); coins (FACTORY GIRLS)

Scene 5: Bucket (THENARDIER); basket, envelope with letter (MME. THENARDIER)

Scene 6: License, tray of flowers (MARGUERITE); two coins, tattered shawl, hankerchief (FANTINE)

Scene 7: Envelope with letter, clay pipe (POLICEMAN)

Scene 8: Chains or handcuffs (CHAMPMATHIEU)

Scene 10: Hospital gown (FANTINE); pillow, blanket or sheet (SISTER SIMPLICITY)

PROPERTIES - ACT TWO

On Stage: Small writing table with chair, pen and ink bottle, mirror, towel, washbasin and pitcher on stand, section of broken "wall." (MARIUS' tenement room)

Table with broken chair, stools, pile of rags, sleeping cot, optional clothesline with torn garments. (THENARDIER's tenement room)

Desk with chair. (JAVERT's office)

Bench (Luxembourg Gardens)

Brought on:
Prologue: Walking stick (cane) (VICTOR H.)
Scene 1: Pamphlet (MARIUS)
Scene 2: Pamphlets (ADELE, HENRI); books, coins, note (MARIUS); another note (AZELMA)
Scene 3: Bread loaf, books (MARIUS)
Scene 4: Blackjack or lead pipe (THENARDIER) -- from under pile of rags
Scene 5: Pocket watch (JAVERT)
Scene 6: Wooden tavern sign
Scene 9: Rifle (HENRI, EPONINE, ADELE); coin (MARIUS)
Scene 10: Barricade, flags, banners, rifles
Scene 11: Shawl (MME. THENARDIER)
Scene 12: Small chair (CHARLOTTE); floor-length robe, cane (VALJEAN); prayer book (MONSEIGNEUR MYRIEL); walking stick (VICTOR H.)

SOUND EFFECTS

Various snippets of mood music, including sparkling waltz, Christmas Carol (can be sung by cast members). Artillery, gunfire, drum roll, police whistles.

LIGHTING

Simple, as suggested in script. However, any innovations are always to the good. For example, area lighting for the individual scenes, a shifting (up or down) of the lights to indicate a new locale, day or night.

A blue cyclorama at the rear of the stage, bordered by a ground row of lights, will enable the production to come up with all manner of effects.

The BIG moment will be the barricade scene. All stops out -- flashing lights to simulate gunfire, bursts of red for artillery, etc.

THE BARRICADE

The important thing is that the "building" not be clumsy or distracting. Actually, a barricade consists of whatever CITIZENS can come up with: chairs, barrels, carts, planks of wood, and the like. However, for a smooth moving in and out of place, have the barricade already "built" in two or more sections.

Another option is to have the barricade "painted on" a scenic flat and slid into place when required. The shadowy lightning and the battle "effects" will cover the deception.

Remember, Victor H. sets the staging tone in the prologue: "Our canvas is one of imagination."

COSTUMES

Special costumes are indicated in text. Whatever you'd come up with for a production of a Charles Dickens' book, will work nicely with "Les Misérables." Do give some care to Cosette's wedding gown.

FLEXIBLE CASTING, DOUBLING

The script has been designed to accommodate almost any requirement. If more female roles are needed, consider this: role of HENRI can be changed to HARRIET; FAUCHELEVENT can become MME. FAUCHELEVENT. Instead of the narrator being Victor Hugo, it can be one of his daughters, LEOPOLDINE. The opening lines of the Act One Prologue will change to: "My name is Leopoldine. I am the daughter of Victor Hugo, a writer. These actors you see here are his creations, etc."

The POLICEMEN: Avoid having the same two actors play the police of Act One and Act Two. It should be a different set for each act.

"Doubles" are easily achieved. What follows is merely a suggestion of what might be managed. For example:

EPONINE - might also portray GIRL #1 or GIRL #2 or GIRL #3

AZELMA - any one of the factory girls, MAGUERITE, SISTER SIMPLICITY

MME. MAGLIORE - COURT SPECTATOR, MLLE. GILLENORMAND, MME. GRIBIER

MONSEIGNEUR MYRIEL - PLAINCLOTHES POLICEMAN, CITIZEN

MME. VICTURNIEN - CITIZEN, COURT SPECTATOR, WEDDING GUEST

BAMATABOIS - CITIZEN, COURT SPECTATOR, WEDDING GUEST, PLAINCLOTHES POLICEMAN, SERGEANT

JUDGE - CITIZEN, PLAINCLOTHES POLICEMAN

PROSECUTOR - CITIZEN, PLAINCLOTHES POLICEMAN, WEDDING GUEST

MME. RONDEAU - CITIZEN, YOUNG WOMAN (ACT TWO)

SISTER SIMPLICITY - MLLE. GILLENORMAND

...and on and on. DOUBLING POSSIBILITIES ARE ALMOST LIMITLESS.

SCENE BREAKDOWN WITH CHARACTERS
FOR REHEARSAL PURPOSES

ACT ONE

Prologue: Open Stage
        Entire Cast

Scene 1: Town street
        Valjean, Mme. Magliore

Scene 2: Cottage of Monseigneur Myriel,
        Monseigneur Myriel, Mlle. Baptistine,
        Valjean, Sergeant, Policeman

Scene 3: Outside the Thenardier Inn
        Mme. Thenardier, Thenardier, Fantine

Scene 4: Factory yard
        Mme. Victurnien, Fauchelevent, Girl #1,
        Girl #2, Girl #3, Fantine

Scene 5: Outside the Thenardier Inn
        Thenardier, Mme. Thenardier

Scene 6: A street
        Marguerite, Javert, Fantine, Bamatabois,
        Young Man, Young Woman

Scene 7: Police headquarters
        Policeman, Javert, Fantine, Valjean

Scene 8: Courtroom
        Judge, Prosecutor, Sergeant, Policeman,
        Champmathieu, Mme. Rondeau, Bibolet,
        Valjean, Spectators

Scene 9: A street
        Mme. Victurnien, Fauchelevent,
        Mme. Gribier

Scene 10: Hospital room
        Fantine, Sister Simplicity, Valjean,
        Javert

ACT TWO

Prologue: Paris
           Victor H., Valjean, Cosette, Marius
Scene 1:   House of Mlle. Gillenormand
           Marius, Mlle. Gillenormand
Scene 2:   Luxembourg Gardens
           Adele, Henri, Marius, Javert,
           Plainclothes Policeman, Valjean, Cosette,
           Charlotte, Azelma, Citizens
Scene 3:   Marius' room
           Marius, Eponine
Scene 4:   Thenardier's room
           Thenardier, Azelma, Valjean,
           Mme. Thenardier
Scene 5:   Javert's office, Police Headquarters
           Javert, Marius
Scene 6:   Thenardier's room
           Thenardier, Mme. Thenardier, Valjean,
           Azelma, Javert
Scene 7:   Luxembourg Gardens
           Marius, Cosette, Valjean
Scene 8:   House of Mlle Gillenormand
           Mlle. Gillenormand, Marius
Scene 9:   Luxembourg Gardens
           Henri, Citizens, Marius, Eponine, Adele
           Cosette, Valjean
Scene 10: The Barricade
           Citizens, Henri, Adele, Marius, Eponine,
           Javert, Valjean, Victor H.
Scene 11: House of Mlle. Gillenormand
           Marius, Charlotte, Mlle. Gillenormand,
           Mme. Thenardier, Cosette
Scene 12: Open stage
           Entire cast

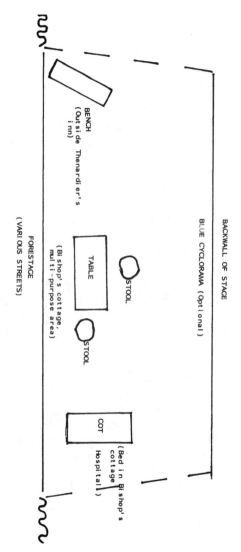

ACT ONE

BACKWALL OF STAGE

BLUE CYCLORAMA (Optional)

BENCH
(Outside Thenardier's
inn)

TABLE

STOOL

STOOL

(Bishop's cottage,
multi-purpose area)

COT

(Bed in Bishop's
cottage
Hospital)

FORESTAGE
(VARIOUS STREETS)

LES MISÉRABLES
SUGGESTED UNIT SETTING

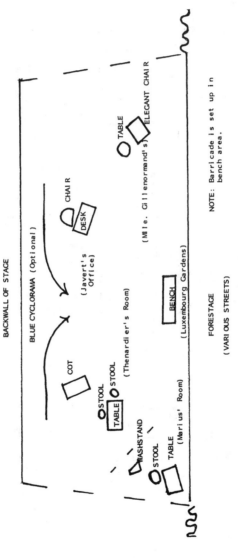

ACT TWO

BACKWALL OF STAGE

BLUE CYCLORAMA (Optional)

CHAIR
DESK
(Javert's Office)

COT

STOOL
TABLE
STOOL
(Thenardier's Room)

WASHSTAND
STOOL
TABLE
(Marius' Room)

TABLE
ELEGANT CHAIR
(Mlle. Gillenormand's)

BENCH
(Luxembourg Gardens)

FORESTAGE
(VARIOUS STREETS)

NOTE: Barricade is set up in bench area.

LES MISÉRABLES

SUGGESTED UNIT SETTING

WHAT PEOPLE ARE SAYING about *Les Misérables*...

"Our school most often does comedy or lighter dramas so this was quite a change. The students involved were very excited to do this classic. Many from the audience commented on how entertaining this drama was. As a director I thought this had a good variety of characters for a drama department with a larger number of students."
Betty Schreiner,
Portland Christian School,
Louisville, Ky.

"A wonderful play that captures the intent of the novel yet is presented in an audience-pleasing manner."
J.D. Gonzales,
Kelloggsville High School,
Grand Rapids, Mich.

"This is an excellent version that works well with limited scenery and staging time. The roles are spread out well, giving many actors a chance to shine. The challenge of the more dramatic roles was appreciated by my cast."
Todd Kelly,
Pottsgrove High School,
Pottstown, Pa.

"This was a very meaningful experience for my students. We focused on the theme of the power of forgiveness and how it can impact a life permanently, as well as the counter theme of vengefulness. The simplicity of our set allowed a stronger focus on the characters, and even our younger audiences were affected by these powerful themes."
Donna Grabill,
Northside Christian School,
St. Petersburg, Fla.

DIRECTOR'S NOTES